moon aged 27

OL

HOROSCOPE AND ASTRAL DIARY

•

VIRGO

foulsham

LONDON • NEW YORK • TORONTO • SYDNEY

foulsham

The Publishing House, Bennetts Close,
Cippenham, Berks SL1 5AP

ISBN 0-572-02103-8

Printed in Great Britain at
Cox & Wyman Ltd, Reading

CONTENTS

OLD MOORE'S HOROSCOPE AND ASTRAL DIARY

Old Moore's Horoscope and Astral Diary represents a major departure from the usual format of publications dedicated to popular Sun-sign astrology. In this book, more attention than ever before has been focused on the discovery of the 'real you', through a wealth of astrological information, presented in an easy to follow and interesting form, and designed to provide a comprehensive insight into your fundamental nature.

The interplay of the Sun and Moon form complex cycles that are brought to bear on each of us in different ways. In the pages that follow I will explain how a knowledge of these patterns in your life can make relationships with others easier and general success more possible. Realising when your mind and body are at their most active or inactive, and at what times your greatest efforts are liable to see you winning through, can be of tremendous importance. In addition, your interaction with other zodiac types is explored, together with a comprehensive explanation of your Sun-sign nature,

In the Astral Diary you will discover a day-to-day reading covering a fifteen-month period. The readings are compiled from solar, lunar and planetary relationships as they bear upon your own zodiac sign. In addition, easy-to-follow graphic charts offer you at a glance an understanding of the way that your personal life-cycles are running; what days are best for maximum effort and when your system is likely to be regenerating.

Because some people want to look deeper into the fascinating world of personal astrology, there is a section of the book allowing a more in-depth appraisal of the all-important zodiac sign that was 'Rising' at the time of your birth. You can also look at your own personal 'Moon Sign' using simple to follow instructions to locate the position of this very significant heavenly body on the day that you were born.

From a simple-to-follow diary section, on to an intimate understanding of the ever-changing child of the solar system that you are, my Horoscope and Astral Diary will allow you to unlock potential that you never even suspected you had.

With the help and guidance of the following pages, Old Moore wishes you a happy and prosperous future.

HERE'S LOOKING AT YOU

A ZODIAC PORTRAIT OF VIRGO
(24th AUGUST - 23rd SEPTEMBER)

Virgo is invariably recognised as being an orderly, neat, tidy and
well co-ordinated sign, its subjects are thought of as being the
sort of people who won't have a single hair out of place. Even
something as innocuous as stains on clothing are said to send
the typical Virgoan into a blind panic, so fastidious are these
people supposed to be concerning every detail. Of course, as with
every other zodiac sign there are Virgoans and Virgoans, though
it has to be said that there is more than a grain of truth is this
description of Mercury's Earth-sign rulership.

In terms of physical stature, the typical Virgo is likely to be
medium in height, with an oval face, clear complexion and especially striking eyes, often bluish in colour. The nose is small and
aquiline and the smile radiates a genuine sincerity.

But what about the person behind the looks, what really
makes you tick as an individual? Being an Earth-sign individual, your outlook on life is likely to be rather conservative.
It is important to you to present the right impression in public,
so that you have a preference for dressing well. You are good in
conversation, ruled as you are by that lord of communication,
Mercury, and yet like all Earth-signs you have a basic quietness
of nature that is as likely to see you choosing the written word,
in place of the spoken one, for your most intimate considerations.

Although you are fairly robust in health, you do have a rather
dodgy nervous system, a fact that means you need to take plenty
of rest. Retreating into the countryside is ideal for you at times
of stress. All too often however you keep pushing and striving for
those objectives that you have set your mind on, a fact that sets
you apart as being quite stubborn, and one that can lead to nervous exhaustion if you do not exercise care. Despite your
generally rude good health, you can be something of a
hypochondriac and take an interest in all matters of health and
hygiene. Anxiety shown concerning the least ailment only serves
to make you burn up yet more nervous energy, and can lead in itself to bouts of illness.

THE INTENTION

You must have been told just how particular Virgo subjects can be, even to the point of being over-critical. At your worst, you are a nitpicker, and this can give the impression that you think yourself to be perfect. In reality, you attempt to establish order in what you view as being a generally chaotic world, and to make all things work in a practical way. Your work is never done, at least that is how it appears to you; and in addition to the need to roll up your sleeves and get stuck into jobs personally, being ruled by Mercury, you also have a wealth of ideas about everything, and no lack of words to communicate them to the world at large. Whilst Gemini (Mercury's other rulership) wants information for its own sake, Virgoans seek to put it to practical use. As a result, others rely on you, and more often than not you are willing to shoulder the burden.

Because Virgo is a mutable sign, there is a suggestion of adaptability. This shows in terms of your ability to fit into existing situations, even if later you have to turn them round to your own point of view. It can seem that you will even seek to improve those situations that are doing quite well left to their own devices and 'Leave it alone' may be an instruction to carry around in your subconscious, if you don't want to upset people who think they are fine as they are. It isn't really your fault; you need to find order and appropriateness in all aspects of your everyday world. Yours is a restless and highly-strung sign, but one that possesses great determination, courage and compassion. You are dutiful. diligent and basically very kind.

YOUR VIRTUES

Those people who know you the best and on upon whom you have bestowed your life-long friendship would have no difficulty finding ways to extol your virtues, after all, are you not always around to help and advise when they need you the most? This is the sort of situation when you show yourself in the best light possible, because you are a born organiser and love to be of assistance. You are often to be found in the background, and don't need to be leading from the front, as would be the case with a Leo or a Sagittarian; and yet your influence in all you undertake is easily felt.

In your efforts to help the world, as well as yourself because nobody can be entirely altruistic, you show diplomacy, tact and shrewdness. On most occasions you act with forethought and do not know the meaning of defeat once your mind is made up. On the way, you avariciously hoover up all the information about life that comes your way, putting each and every fact to good use sooner or later. Anything and everything is grist to the mill of knowledge that grinds away constantly inside your mind. Virgoans are at their best in an occupation which allows full use of the mental faculties at their disposal, yet because the sign of the Virgin is of the Earth element, it is not unusual to find individuals from this part of the zodiac tilling the good earth for a living, or at least tending a flower bed at the weekends.

Perhaps your greatest virtue, and it is one that many astrologers leave out, is your ingenuity, which together with a good intuitive quality and the ability to work hard , can see you building a secure and stable position in life for yourself.

YOUR VICES

It is the essence of the universe that for every plus, there must be a minus. Astrology, like everything else, conforms to this principle, and nowhere is it better exemplified than in the mentally-motivated but loamy depths of Virgo. Let's face it; at your worst you can be tedious and argumentative, interfering and downright bloody-minded. It isn't that you set out to be this way, it's simply a natural consequence of your need to see everything running smoothly. The problem is that in your heart of hearts you don't really believe that anyone else can do things as well as you can. Because you have a natural tendency to gather around you the sort of people that either need your personal brand of 'help', or at least individuals who have observed and felt your kind heart, all is usually well. The problems arise when, as a natural consequence of living in a world full of other people, you come across those infuriating types who think they know better than you do. Woe betide them, because once you decide to dig your heels in, you can be as stubborn as a mule and as tenacious as a bulldog. All the same, you can be a little unreasonable yourself on occasions and so perhaps a bit more patience on your part would not be a bad thing.

Your nervous system is always working overtime, a fact that can be responsible for uncharacteristic displays of surly bad temper, particularly if you happen to think there is something physically wrong with you, which is quite often. This is when you really come into your own, worrying away at a particular point until everyone around flees from the room in frustration or anger. Take heart though; the whole world knows that underneath it all you have a heart as big as a bus, and they won't bear a grudge - even if you sometimes do!

LIVING A HAPPY LIFE

In your case there are a few definite pointers, the observation of which, whilst not guaranteed to make you rich or famous, could easily lead to a more contented existence. First of all, remember that you are what you eat. The happiest Virgoans seem to be those that avoid animal based products as much as possible; the simpler the fare, the better, seems to the the motto. This stems from the fact that you are born under the Earth element, indicating that the produce of the earth suits your constitution best. Born as you were in the late summer, the fruits of nature's larder have a particular part to play in keeping you healthy. And once you have your diet right, you next need to build a world where worries are kept to a minimum. Remember that your aspirations can be out of tune with your needs and that today's boredom can be tomorrow's security. In other words, what you want out of life may not be the same as what you need.

Get plenty of outdoor exercise, looking at nature, and climbing hills as often as you can. Too often, Virgoans are inclined to stay close to home, which may suit your retreatist tendencies but does nothing towards allowing you the communication that is so important in keeping you healthy from a mental point of view. When you are forced to stay close to your abode, cultivate as wide a circle of friends as you can manage and learn to accept each of them for what they are, interfering in their lives only when you are asked. It isn't that you mean to take people over, merely that you are just so much more organised than they are.

Make certain that there is always something going on to stimulate your active, busy mind; an association with societies or social groups is good. You can be of great use to others, with your verbal dexterity and organising skills, so that any charity would probably be grateful to have you around. But above all, remember that you are not half so confident regarding yourself as you sometimes give the impression of being. Learn to laugh at your own faults and you will like yourself a whole lot better.

WHAT'S RISING

YOUR RISING SIGN AND PERSONALITY

Perhaps you have come across this term 'Rising Sign' when looking at other books on astrology and may have been somewhat
puzzled as to what it actually means. To those not accustomed
to astrological jargon it could sound somewhat technical and
mysterious, though in fact, in terms of your own personal birth
chart, it couldn't be simpler. The Rising Sign is simply that part
of the zodiac occupying the eastern horizon at the time of your
birth. Because it is a little more difficult to discover than your
sun-sign, many writers of popular astrology have tended to
ignore it, which is a great shame, because, together with the
Sun, your Rising Sign is the single most important factor in
terms of setting your personality. So much so, that no appraisal
of your astrological nature could be complete without it.

Your Rising Sign, also known as your 'Ascendant' or 'Ascen-
ding Sign' plays a great part in your looks - yes, astrology can
even predict what you are going to be like physically. In fact,
this is a very interesting point, because there appears to be a tie-
in between astrology and genetics. Professional Astrologers for
centuries have noted the close relationship that often exists between the astrological birth chart of parents and those of their
offspring, so that, if you look like your Mother or Father, chances
are that there is a close astrological tie-up. Rising signs especially appear to be handed down through families.

The first impression that you get, in an astrological sense,
upon meeting a stranger, is not related to their sun-sign but to
the zodiac sign that was rising at the moment they came into the
world. The Rising Sign is particularly important because it
modifies the way that you display your Sun-sign to the world at
large. A good example of this might be that of Britain's best-
known ex- Prime minister, Margaret Thatcher. This dynamic
and powerful lady is a Libran by Sun-sign placing, indicating a
light-hearted nature, pleasure loving and very flexible.
However, Mrs Thatcher has Scorpio as her Rising Sign, bringing
a steely determination and a tremendous capacity for work. It
also bestows an iron will and the power to thrive under pressure.

Here lies the true importance of the Rising Sign, for Mr
Thatcher almost certainly knows a woman who most other

people do not. The Rising Sign is a protective shell, and not until we know someone quite well do we start to discover the Sun-sign nature that hides within this often tough outer coat of astrological making. Your Rising Sign also represents your basic self-image, the social mask that is often so useful; and even if you don't think that you conform to the interpretation of your Ascendant, chances are that other people will think that you do.

The way that an individual looks, walks, sits and generally presents themselves to the world is all down to the Rising Sign. For example, a person possessed of Gemini Rising is apt to be very quick, energetic in all movements, deliberate in mannerisms and with a cheerful disposition. A bearer of a Taurean Ascendant on the other hand would probably not be so tall, more solid generally, quieter in aspect and calmer in movement. Once you come to understand the basics of astrology it is really very easy to pick out the Rising Signs of people that you come across, even though the Sun-sign is often more difficult to pin down. Keep an eye open for the dynamic and positive Aries Rising individual, or the retiring, shy but absolutely magnetic quality of of the Piscean Ascendant. Of course, in astrology, nothing is quite that simple. The position of a vast array of heavenly bodies at the time of birth also has to be taken into account, particularly that of the Moon and the inner planets Mercury and Venus. Nevertheless a knowledge of your Rising sign can be an invaluable aid in getting to know what really makes you tick as an individual.

To ascertain the exact degree of your Rising sign takes a little experience and recourse to some special material. However, I have evolved a series of tables that will enable you to discover at a glance what your Rising Sign is likely to be. All you need to know is the approximate time of your birth. At the back of the book you will find the necessary table related to your Sun-sign. Simply look down the left-hand column until you find your approximate time of birth, am or pm. Now scan across the top of the table to the place where your date of birth is shown. Look for the square where the two pieces of information connect and there is your Rising Sign. Now that you know what your Rising Sign is, read on, and learn even more about the fascinating interplay of astrological relationship.

VIRGO WITH VIRGO RISING

A doubling up of the qualities of Virgo is a very powerful package indeed and indicates to the world 'what you see is what you get.' This means that all the typical gains and losses of the Virgo incarnation are yours for the taking. You look after your own affairs very well, and probably everyone else's too. In love you are ardent and sincere and most people should have a very good idea of what to expect from you. Mentality is your motivating factor and that busy, inquisitive mind of yours is constantly on the go, searching for new material that you can assimilate into your life.

Now this is where choice comes in. Have you ever seen the television comedy series where the actress, Patricia Routledge plays the indefatigable Mrs Bucket? Here is the sign of Virgo at it's worst. Snobbish, house proud to the point of absurdity, interfering, calculating and over-anxious about impressions. If you choose one side of the fence, here is your role-model. Should you desire to come down on the other side however, you can opt instead for a steady, interesting life; anxious to serve when you can and happy to accept the rest of humanity for what it is. The choice is yours!

VIRGO WITH LIBRA RISING

Hardly the typical Virgo subject, you are much more likely to exude the qualities of your rising sign Libra. This is a happy combination, for whilst Virgo is inclined to take itself a little too seriously on occasions, Libra is fun loving, easy going, extravagant and certainly more socially orientated than Virgo. With your disarming charm (and probably more than your fair share of good looks) you approach the world with great sensitivity to the needs of others

Your sense of identity comes from others, and you are very susceptible to what your friends and relatives have to say. In some ways this is an admirable thing, though you should also take time out for self-study, and for coming to terms with your own deeper self. There is an inherent confusion about socialising because Libra always wants to be with others, whilst Virgo is often happy to be alone. You do need to show the more assertive qualities that lie deep within your nature and to recognise that just a little of the loyalty that you show to others could be turned back in your own direction.

VIRGO WITH SCORPIO RISING

Here the Virgoan qualities of discrimination and rational analysis combine with Scorpio's powerful intuition to create an individual who does not miss a trick. It would be very rare for you to overlook the smallest detail. Nevertheless, the judgements that you make regarding others can sometimes be a little harsh. It has to be said that your first impressions are usually correct, but remember that even you can be wrong and that words, once uttered, cannot be un-said. You are sensitive to the needs of others in a practical way, which is why so many of your astrological brothers and sisters work in the medical profession. In personal relationships you are passionate and faithful - occasionally too much for your own good.

You may well have some very definite ideas about the world, particularly from a political point of view. In many respects you are the perfect humanitarian, just as long as humanity wants what you think is best for them. Like all Scorpio-tinged people, you don't take very kindly to opposition. However, such is your determination that you can do much good for yourself and the people whose lives you touch.

VIRGO WITH SAGITTARIUS RISING

Blessed with an abundant store of healthy optimism, there is little doubt that some of the more negative traits of the Virgo nature are tempered or even eradicated by the cocktail presented when Jupiter ruled Sagittarius is in the ascendant. You often look on the brighter side of life, always seeking to establish a positive way in which you can view things. Being adaptable and communicative, you are always willing to learn, can easily keep more than one occupation going and are quite good at convincing other people of your point of view.

It is true that you are always looking for some greater meaning to many of life's complexities, and others find you restless to have around on occasion. They always forgive you though because you can be relied upon to have something interesting to say on any occasion. Of course, under-pinning this devil-take-care attitude is the hard, realistic Virgo subject, which is why you are likely to be more successful than the typical Archer might be, though despite Virgo's presence, you can spread yourself too thinly on occasions and need to discover what you really ought to be doing with your life.

VIRGO WITH CAPRICORN RISING

A double helping of the Earth element, as with all other astrological possibilities, has its pluses and minuses. You certainly have the ability to actualise your desires through sheer hard work, determination and effort. It's possible for you to see through the fog of everyday concerns to the heart of almost any situation and to work out instinctively the best course of action to take. In addition you make a very firm friend and are extremely trustworthy.

One of the problems that you may encounter, is a tendency to take yourself, and possibly life as a whole, a little too seriously, running the risk of alienating yourself from much 'lighter' sorts of people, who in reality are exactly the folk that you need around you. Worry is something that you should learn to come to terms with, perhaps by cultivating the simple belief in tomorrow looking after its own problems and also by realising that you cannot change the nature of the world as a whole, no matter how hard you may try. You like to learn and to plan and it is important for you to keep on the move, constantly searching for your own El Dorado. Nobody should knock this side of your nature though, because you often find it!

VIRGO WITH AQUARIUS RISING

There is something a little unusual about this combination of signs, in fact it might be said that you are far from run of the mill yourself. You have your share of eccentric little quirks that others find difficult to understand. Despite this you are kind-hearted and willing to go to almost any lengths to be of assistance. With a genuine desire to see your fellow men and women prosper in their own lives, the presence of Aquarius in your make-up creates an altruistic and philanthropic nature. A problem here is that being so truthful about everything yourself, you are inclined to believe that the rest of humanity is the same, which is why you can be so frequently disappointed when you discover that they are not. Even this may not be too much of a let-down, considering that you are not the world's most emotionally motivated individual anyway. Your biggest problem may be when it comes to intimacy, because you are far happier to be skating over the surface of deep water, in addition to which you tend to subject everything in life to the sharp knife of rational intellect.

VIRGO WITH PISCES RISING

The positive aspects of this combination are born of your wonderful sensitivity to others and the sacrifices that you are willing to make on their behalf. Your kindness is laudable and you are usually willing to take others as you find them, not as you would wish them to be. All of this makes you a very popular person and it is only a pity that you cannot also be more discriminating and selective in your choice of friends and associates.

The secret seems to lie in distancing yourself from people and situations emotionally. Not an easy thing for you to do when guilt trips are the inevitable outcome. Because you are probably a fairly retiring type, there are occasions when you seem to be left at the starting post in practical matters, yet in personal relationships there are few to equal you and it is in this sphere of life that you really do come into your own. Even this can be a problem on occasions because you are inclined to 'cling' so you do need to keep track of your own identity and needs on the way.

VIRGO WITH ARIES RISING

In one respect at least, you are typical of the sign of Virgo; specifically in your desire to be constantly busy. This might be where the similarity ends however, since you are much more impatient than the Virgin is usually considered to be, in addition to manifesting a greater degree of brashness, courage and general force of character. You are a force to be reckoned with, holding the cool and methodical thinking of an Earth sign individual, backed up by all the power of the most dynamic of the Fire signs. There is little that you set your mind on that you cannot achieve, partly because you are realistic.

You can be guaranteed to have your say, and as far as work is concerned, you simply have to be left alone to get on with things in your own sweet way. Some people might consider that you are a bit of a 'know it all', and they would probably be right, because generally speaking you do! Watch out for a tendency to be rather too brusque for your own good, making a few enemies on the way, but remain proud of your scrupulous honesty and your ability to sort out any dilemma at a lightning speed.

VIRGO WITH TAURUS RISING

Despite this being a double helping of the Earth element, with Taurus Rising it is apt to play down some of the more hard-edged qualities of Virgo. The combination tends to throw up a nature that can be observed as being less highly-strung than the typical Virgoan might be and may replace this with a more sensually motivated character, quite typical of the Bull. Thus you may show a fondness for good food and drink, plenty of sleep and long hours spent in the luxury of a deep bath.

Creativity is important, and so is the need to shine in your own right. Aided by Virgo, you may show signs of being a potentially good writer, or through Taurus, a painter. Others are almost certain to sit up and take notice of the unique blend that these two signs tend to create and, superficially at least, you can give much back in terms of natural warmth and affection. Below the surface things might be different, because there is an inherent coldness that will need to be controlled on occasions. If anything, you can be a little too sensible, for your own good and that of the world at large.

VIRGO WITH GEMINI RISING

Mercury, the planet of communication, rules both these signs, so you have a double helping of the communication skills that are so much a part of your Sun-sign. Nobody with a Gemini Ascendant is going to take themselves as seriously as the typical Virgoan might and so there is a 'lightness' of nature in your make-up that gives you extra charisma. Your sense of humour and timing are second to none and it isn't at all difficult for you to make an impression. There are a multitude of acquaintances in your life, though probably only a handful of really close, personal friends.

The combination of Gemini's inspiration, quick thinking and verbal dexterity, together with Virgoan persistence and concentration is a magical mixture. This can assure you of the best of both worlds, for you possess a working knowledge of the world as a whole, though you can specialise quite successfully too. The breezy personality that everyone knows you for may well mask a much more sensitive core. Despite your sociability, you prefer others to come and visit you, in a home which may well reflect typical Virgo pride in surroundings.

VIRGO WITH CANCER RISING

The critical and somewhat analytical faculties of Virgo are slightly diminished and softened with this Rising Sign. The Cancerian side of you tends to accept people the way they are, without trying to change them in any way. You can be a typical Cancerian fuss-pot though, wanting to mother everyone and sort them out generally. Both signs feel they know what is best for other people. In reality, the world could do with more people of your sort; you would excel in the medical profession, or anywhere that you can serve human need.

In terms of personality it is possible that you are sometimes too shy for your own good, and you are also highly emotional. Like all Crabs you hide your true feeling behind a crusty shell and don't really care for people probing too much. You might make a good writer and would be great at critical analysis of any sort. It could be hard to keep your mind working in a genuinely logical way, but then you are so intuitive, you probably don't have to. Don't be ashamed to find so much tenderness within yourself. Remember that it is a gift to be shared with others.

VIRGO WITH LEO RISING

As with all Leo Rising people, it is your way to make a big impression on others, such is your warm, magnanimous, self-promoting nature. Most people would never guess that you are a Virgo, unless they get to know you very well. In fact the two signs don't really work together all that well, indicating that you may sometimes overdo the qualities of one sign, to the detriment of the other. An easy blend is rare, though when you do achieve it, the world can revel in the sunny and playful aspects of the Lion and the practical approach of Virgo. In an emergency you are second to none and in your approach to other people you are generous to a fault, even if it means going without something yourself.

Unpredictability is possibly your stumbling block, as it is to anyone ruled predominantly by Mercury. In your case the trait is more emphasised and some people will find it difficult to come to terms with you because of this slight flaw in your nature. You are a hard worker and can quite easily dedicate yourself to a career or a cause. Most of all, you hate beng told what to do.

VIRGO
IN LOVE AND FRIENDSHIP

WANT TO KNOW HOW WELL YOU GET ON WITH OTHER ZODIAC SIGNS?

THE TABLES BELOW DEAL WITH LOVE AND FRIENDSHIP

THE MORE HEARTS THERE ARE AGAINST ANY SIGN OF THE ZODIAC, THE BETTER THE CHANCE OF CUPID'S DART SCORING A DIRECT HIT.

THE SMILES OF FRIENDSHIP DISPLAY HOW WELL YOU WORK OR ASSOCIATE WITH ALL THE OTHER SIGNS OF THE ZODIAC.

Hearts	Sign	Smiles
♥ ♥ ♥ ♥	ARIES	☺ ☺ ☺
♥ ♥ ♥ ♥ ♥	TAURUS	☺ ☺ ☺ ☺ ☺
♥ ♥ ♥	GEMINI	☺ ☺ ☺
♥	CANCER	☺ ☺
♥ ♥	LEO	☺ ☺ ☺
♥ ♥ ♥ ♥ ♥	VIRGO	☺ ☺ ☺ ☺
♥ ♥	LIBRA	☺ ☺
♥ ♥ ♥	SCORPIO	☺ ☺ ☺
♥ ♥ ♥	SAGITTARIUS	☺ ☺ ☺
♥ ♥ ♥ ♥ ♥	CAPRICORN	☺ ☺ ☺ ☺ ☺
♥ ♥	AQUARIUS	☺ ☺ ☺
♥ ♥ ♥	PISCES	☺ ☺

THE MOON AND YOUR DAY-TO-DAY LIFE

Look up at the sky on cloudless nights and you are almost certain to see the Earth's closest neighbour in space, engaged in her intricate and complicated relationship with the planet upon which we live. The Moon isn't very large, in fact only a small fraction of the size of the Earth, but it is very close to us in spatial terms, and here lies the reason why the Moon probably has more of a part to play in your day-to-day life than any other body in space.

It is fair to say in astrological terms that if the Sun and Planets represent the hour and minute hands regulating your character swings and mood changes, the Moon is a rapidly sweeping second hand, governing emotions especially, but touching practically every aspect of your life.

Although the Moon moves so quickly, and maintains a staggeringly complex orbital relationship with the Earth, no book charting the possible ups and downs of your daily life could be complete without some reference to lunar action. For this reason I have included a number of the more important lunar cycles that you can observe within your own life, and also give you the opportunity to discover which zodiac sign the Moon occupied when you were born. Follow the instructions below and you will soon have a far better idea of where astrological cycles come from, and the part they play in your life.

SUN MOON CYCLES

The first lunar cycle deals with the relationship that the Moon keeps with your Sun sign. I have made the fluctuations of this pattern easy for you to understand by means of a simple cyclic graph. It appears on the first page of each 'Your Month At A Glance', under the title 'Highs and Lows'. The graph displays the lunar cycle and you will soon learn to understand how its movements have a bearing on your level of energy and your abilities. Once you recognise the patterns, you can work within them, making certain that your maximum efforts are expounded at the most opportune time.

MOON AGE CYCLES

Looking at the second lunar pattern that helps to make you feel the way you do, day-to-day, involves a small amount of work on your part to establish how you slot into the rhythm. However, since Moon Age cycles are one of the most potent astrological forces at work in your life, the effort is more than worthwhile.

This cycle refers to the way that the date of your birth fits into the Moon Phase pattern. Because of the complex relationship of the Earth and the Moon, we see the face of the lunar disc change throughout a period of roughly one month. The time between one New Moon (this is when there is no Moon to be seen) to the next New Moon, is about 29 days. Between the two the Moon would have seemed larger each night until the lunar disc was Full; it would then start to recede back towards New again. We call this cycle the Moon Age Cycle and classify the day of the New Moon as day 0. Full Moon occurs on day 15 with the last day of the cycle being either day 28 or day 29, dependent on the complicated motions of the combined Earth and Moon.

If you know on what Moon Age Day you were born, then you also know how you fit into the cycle. You would monitor the changes of the cycle as more or less tension in your body, an easy or a strained disposition, good or bad temper and so forth. In order to work out your Moon Age Day follow the steps below:

STEP 1: Look at the two New Moon Tables on pages 23 and 24. Down the left hand column you will see every year from 1902 to 1994 listed, and the months of the year appear across the top. Where the year of your birth and the month that you were born coincide, the figure shown indicates the date of the month on which New Moon occurred.

STEP 2: You need to pick the New Moon that occurred prior to your day of birth, so if your birthday falls at the beginning of the month, you may have to refer to the New Moon from the previous month. Once you have established the nearest New Moon prior to your birthday, (and of course in the correct year), all you have to do is count forward to your birthday. (Don't forget that the day of the New Moon is classed as 0.) As an example, if your were born on March 22nd 1962, the last New Moon before your birthday would have occurred on 6th March 1962. Counting forward from 6 to 22 would mean that you were born on Moon Age

Day 16. If your Moon Phase Cycle crosses the end of February, don't forget to check whether or not you were born in a Leap Year. If so you will have to compensate for that fact.

HOW TO USE MOON AGE DAYS

Once you know your Moon Age Day, you can refer to the Diary section of the book, because there, on each day of the year, you will see that the Moon Age Day is listed. The day in each cycle that conforms to your own Moon Age monthly birthday should find you in a positive and optimistic frame of mind Your emotions are likely to be settled and your thinking processes clear and concise. There are other important days that you will want to know about on this cycle, and to make matters simpler I have compiled an easy to follow table on pages 25 and 26. Quite soon you will get to know which Moon Age Days influence you, and how.

Of course Moon Age Cycles, although specific to your own date of birth, also run within the other astrological patterns that you will find described in this book. So, for example, if your Moon Age Day coincided with a particular day of the month, but everything else was working to the contrary, you might be wise to delay any particularly monumental effort until another, more generally favourable, day. Sometimes cycles run together and occasionally they do not; this is the essence of astrological prediction.

YOUR MOON SIGN

Once you have established on what Moon Age Day you were born, it isn't too difficult to also discover what zodiac sign the Moon occupied on the day of your birth. Although the Moon is very small in size compared to some of the solar system's larger bodies, it is very close indeed to the Earth and this seems to give it a special astrological significance. This is why there are many cycles and patterns associated with the Moon that have an important part to play in the lives of every living creature on the face of our planet, Of all the astrological patterns associated with the Moon that have a part to play in your life, none is more potent than those related to the zodiac position of the Moon at birth. Many of the most intimate details of your personal make-up are related to your Moon Sign, and we will look at these now.

HOW TO DISCOVER YOUR MOON SIGN

The Moon moves through each sign of the zodiac in only two to three days. It also has a rather complicated orbital relationship with the Earth; for these reasons it can be difficult to work out what your Zodiac Moon Sign is. However, having discovered your Moon Age Day you are half way towards finding your Moon Sign, and in order to do so, simply follow the steps below:

STEP 1: Make sure that you have a note of your date of birth and also your Moon Age Day.

STEP 2: Look at Zodiac Moon Sign Table 1 on page 27. Find the month of your birth across the top of the table, and your date of birth down the left. Where the two converge you will see a letter. Make a note of the letter that relates to you.

STEP 3: Now turn to Zodiac Moon Sign Table 2 on pages 28 and 30. Look for your Moon Age Day across the top of the tables and the letter that you have just discoverd down the left side. Where the two converge you will see a zodiac sign. The Moon occupied this zodiac sign on the day of your birth.

PLEASE NOTE: The Moon can change signs at any time of the day or night, and the signs listed in this book are generally applicable for 12 noon on each day. If you were born near the start or the end of a particular Zodiac Moon Sign, it is worth reading the character descriptions of adjacent signs. These are listed pages 30to 35. So much of your nature is governed by the Moon at the time of your birth that it should be fairly obvious wich one of the profiles relates to you.

YOUR ZODIAC MOON SIGN EXPLAINED

You will find a profile of all Zodiac Moon Signs on pages 30 to 35, showing in yet another way astrology helps to make you into the individual that you are. In each month in the Astral Diary, in addition to your Moon Age Day, you can also discover your Zodiac Moon Sign birthday (that day when the Moon occupies the same zodiac sign as it did when you were born). At these times you are in the best postion to be emotionally steady and to make the sort of decisions that have real, lasting value.

NEW MOON TABLE

YEAR	JAN	FEB	MAR	APR	MAY	JUN	JUL	AUG	SEP	OCT	NOV	DEC
1902	9	8	9	8	7	6	5	3	2	1/30	29	29
1903	27	26	28	27	26	25	24	22	21	20	19	18
1904	17	15	17	16	15	14	14	12	10	18	8	8
1905	6	5	5	4	3	2	2/31	30	28	28	26	26
1906	24	23	24	23	22	21	20	19	18	17	16	15
1907	14	12	14	12	11	10	9	8	7	6	5	5
1908	3	2	3	2	1/30	29	28	27	25	25	24	24
1909	22	20	21	20	19	17	17	15	14	14	13	12
1910	11	9	11	9	9	7	6	5	3	2	1	1/30
1911	29	28	30	28	28	26	25	24	22	21	20	20
1912	18	17	19	18	17	16	15	13	12	11	9	9
1913	7	6	7	6	5	4	3	2/31	30	29	28	27
1914	25	24	26	24	24	23	22	21	19	19	17	17
1915	15	14	15	13	13	12	11	10	9	8	7	6
1916	5	3	5	3	2	1/30	30	29	27	27	26	25
1917	24	22	23	22	20	19	18	17	15	15	14	13
1918	12	11	12	11	10	8	8	6	4	4	3	2
1919	1/31	-	2/31	30	29	27	27	25	23	23	22	21
1920	21	19	20	18	18	16	15	14	12	12	10	10
1921	9	8	9	8	7	6	5	3	2	1/30	29	29
1922	27	26	28	27	26	25	24	22	21	20	19	18
1923	17	15	17	16	15	14	14	12	10	10	8	8
1924	6	5	5	4	3	2	2/31	30	28	28	26	26
1925	24	23	24	23	22	21	20	19	18	17	16	15
1926	14	12	14	12	11	10	9	8	7	6	5	5
1927	3	2	3	2	1/30	29	28	27	25	25	24	24
1928	21	19	21	20	19	18	17	16	14	14	12	12
1929	11	9	11	9	9	7	6	5	3	2	1	1/30
1930	29	28	30	28	28	26	25	24	22	20	20	19
1931	18	17	19	18	17	16	15	13	12	11	9	9
1932	7	6	7	6	5	4	3	2/31	30	29	2	27
1933	25	24	26	24	24	23	22	21	19	19	17	17
1934	15	14	15	13	13	12	11	10	9	8	7	6
1935	5	3	5	3	2	1/30	30	29	27	27	26	25
1936	24	22	23	21	20	19	18	17	15	15	14	13
1937	12	11	12	12	10	8	8	6	4	4	3	2
1938	1/31	-	2/31	30	29	27	27	25	23	23	22	21
1939	20	19	20	19	19	17	16	15	13	12	11	10
1940	9	8	9	7	7	6	5	4	2	1/30	29	28
1941	27	26	27	26	26	24	24	22	21	20	19	18
1942	16	15	16	15	15	13	13	12	10	10	8	8
1943	6	4	6	4	4	2	2	1/30	29	29	27	27
1944	25	24	24	22	22	20	20	18	17	17	15	15
1945	14	12	14	12	11	10	9	8	6	6	4	4
1946	3	2	3	2	1/30	29	28	26	25	24	23	23
1947	21	19	21	20	19	18	17	16	14	14	12	12

NEW MOON TABLE

YEAR	JAN	FEB	MAR	APR	MAY	JUN	JUL	AUG	SEP	OCT	NOV	DEC
1948	11	9	11	9	9	7	6	5	3	2	1	1/30
1949	29	27	29	28	27	26	25	24	23	21	20	19
1950	18	16	18	17	17	15	15	13	12	11	9	9
1951	7	6	7	6	6	4	4	2	1	1/30	29	28
1952	26	25	25	24	23	22	23	20	29	28	27	27
1953	15	14	15	13	13	11	11	9	8	8	6	6
1954	5	3	5	3	2	1/30	29	28	27	26	25	25
1955	24	22	24	22	21	20	19	17	16	15	14	14
1956	13	11	12	11	10	8	8	6	4	4	2	2
1957	1/30	-	1/31	29	29	27	27	25	23	23	21	21
1958	19	18	20	19	18	17	16	15	13	12	11	10
1959	9	7	9	8	7	6	6	4	3	2/31	30	29
1960	27	26	27	26	26	24	24	22	21	20	19	18
1961	16	15	16	15	14	13	12	11	10	9	8	7
1962	6	5	6	5	4	2	1/31	30	28	28	27	26
1963	25	23	25	23	23	21	20	19	17	17	15	15
1964	14	13	14	12	11	10	9	7	6	5	4	4
1965	3	1	2	1	1/30	29	28	26	25	24	22	22
1966	21	19	21	20	19	18	17	16	14	14	12	12
1967	10	9	10	9	8	7	7	5	4	3	2	1/30
1968	29	28	29	28	27	26	25	24	23	22	21	20
1969	1 9	17	18	16	15	14	13	12	11	10	9	9
1970	7	6	7	6	6	4	4	2	1	1/30	29	28
1971	26	25	26	25	24	22	22	20	19	19	18	17
1972	15	14	15	13	13	11	11	9	8	8	6	6
1973	5	4	5	3	2	1/30	29	28	27	26	25	25
1974	24	22	24	22	21	20	19	17	16	15	14	14
1975	12	11	12	11	11	9	9	7	5	5	3	3
1976	1/31	29	30	29	29	27	27	25	23	23	21	21
1977	19	18	19	18	18	16	16	14	13	12	11	10
1978	9	7	9	7	7	5	5	4	2	2/31	30	29
1979	27	26	27	26	26	24	24	22	21	20	19	18
1980	16	15	16	15	14	13	12	11	10	9	8	7
1981	6	4	6	4	4	2	1/31	29	28	27	26	26
1982	25	23	24	23	21	21	20	19	17	17	15	15
1983	14	13	14	13	12	11	10	8	7	6	4	4
1984	3	1	2	1	1/30	29	28	26	25	24	22	22
1985	21	19	21	20	19	18	17	16	14	14	12	12
1986	10	9	10	9	8	7	7	5	4	3	2	1/30
1987	29	28	29	28	27	26	25	24	23	22	21	20
1988	19	17	18	16	15	14	13	12	11	10	9	9
1989	7	6	7	6	5	3	3	1/31	29	29	28	28
1990	26	25	26	25	24	22	22	20	19	18	17	17
1991	15	14	15	13	13	11	11	9	8	8	6	6
1992	4	3	4	3	2	1/30	29	28	26	25	24	24
1993	24	22	24	22	21	20	19	17	16	15	14	14
1994	11	10	12	11	10	9	8	7	5	5	3	2

24

MOON AGE QUICK REFERENCE TABLE

SIGNIFICANT MOON AGE DAYS

YOUR OWN MOON AGE DAY	+ Days	- Days	* Days
0	4, 6, 12, 14, 19, 21, 25, 28	9, 16, 23	0
1	5, 7, 13, 15, 20, 22, 26, 29	10, 17, 24	1
2	0, 6, 8, 14, 16, 21, 23, 27	11, 18, 25	2
3	1, 7, 9, 15, 17, 22, 24, 28	12, 19, 26	3
4	2, 8, 10, 16, 18, 23, 25, 29	13, 20, 27	4
5	0, 3, 4, 9, 11, 17, 19, 24, 26	14, 21, 28	5
6	1, 4, 5, 10, 12, 18, 20, 25, 27	15, 22, 29	6
7	2, 5, 11, 13, 19, 21, 26, 28	0, 16, 23	7
8	3, 6, 12, 14, 20, 22, 27, 29	1, 17, 24	8
9	0, 4, 7, 13, 15, 21, 23, 28	2, 18, 25	9
10	1, 5, 8, 14, 16, 22, 24, 29	3, 19, 26	10
11	0, 2, 6, 9, 15, 17, 23, 25	4, 20, 27	11
12	1, 3, 7, 10, 16, 18, 24, 26	5, 21, 28	12
13	2, 4, 8, 11, 17, 19, 25, 27	6, 22, 29	13
14	3, 5, 9, 12, 18, 20, 26, 28	0, 7, 23	14
15	4, 6, 10, 13, 19, 21, 27, 29	1, 8, 24	15
16	0, 5, 7, 11, 14, 20, 22, 28	2, 9, 25	16
17	1, 6, 8, 12, 15, 21, 23, 29	3, 10, 26	17
18	0, 2, 7, 9, 13, 16, 22, 24	4, 11, 27	18
19	1, 3, 8, 10, 14, 17, 23, 25	5, 12, 28	19
20	2,4, 9, 11, 15, 18, 24, 26	6, 13, 29	20
21	3, 5, 10, 12, 16, 19, 25, 27	0, 7, 14	21
22	4, 6, 11, 13, 17, 20, 26, 28	1, 8, 15	22
23	5, 7, 12, 14, 18, 21, 27, 29	2, 9, 16	23
24	0, 6, 8, 13, 15, 19, 22, 28	3, 10, 17	24
25	1, 7, 9, 14, 16, 20, 23, 29	4, 11, 18	25
26	0, 2, 8, 10, 15, 17, 21, 24,	5, 12, 19	26
27	1, 3, 9, 11, 16, 18, 22, 25	6, 13, 20	27
28	2, 4, 10, 12, 17, 19, 23, 26	7, 14, 21	28
29	3, 5, 11, 13, 18, 20, 24, 27	8, 15, 22	29

MOON AGE QUICK REFERENCE TABLE

The table opposite will allow you to plot the significant days on the Moon Age Day Cycle and to monitor the way they have a bearing on your own life. You will find an explanation of the Moon Age Cycles on pages 20 - 22. Once you know your own Moon Age Day, you can find it in the left-hand column of the table opposite, To the right of your Moon Age Day you will observe a series of numbers; these appear under three headings. + Days, - Days and * Days.

If you look at the Diary section of the book, immediately to the right of each day and date, the Moon Age Day number is listed. The Quick Reference Table allows you to register which Moon Age Days are significant to you. For example: if your own Moon Age Day is 5, each month you should put a + in the Diary section against Moon Age Days 0, 3, 4, 9, 11, 17, 19, 24, and 26. Jot down a - against Moon Age Days 14, 21 and 28, and a * against Moon Age Day 5. You can now follow your own personal Moon Age Cycle every day of the year.

+ Days are periods when the Moon Age Cycle is in tune with your own Moon Age Day. At this time life should be more harmonious and your emotions are likely to be running smoothly. These are good days for making decisions.

- Days find the Moon Age Cycle out of harmony with your own Moon Age Day. Avoid taking chances at these times and take life reasonably steady. Confrontation would not make sense.

* Days occur only once each Moon Age Cycle, and represent your own Moon Age Day. Such times should be excellent for taking the odd chance and for moving positively towards your objectives in life. On those rare occasions where a * day coincides with your lunar high, you would really be looking at an exceptional period and could afford to be quite bold and adventurous in your approach to life.

MOON ZODIAC SIGN TABLE 1

Month	Jan	Feb	Mar	Apr	May	Jun	Jul	Aug	Sep	Oct	Nov	Dec
1	A	D	F	J	M	O	R	U	X	a	e	i
2	A	D	G	J	M	P	R	U	X	a	e	i
3	A	D	G	J	M	P	S	V	X	a	e	m
4	A	D	G	J	M	P	S	V	Y	b	f	m
5	A	D	G	J	M	P	S	V	Y	b	f	n
6	A	D	G	J	M	P	S	V	Y	b	f	n
7	A	D	G	J	M	P	S	V	Y	b	f	n
8	A	D	G	J	M	P	S	V	Y	b	f	n
9	A	D	G	J	M	P	S	V	Y	b	f	n
10	A	E	G	J	M	P	S	V	Y	b	f	n
11	B	E	G	K	M	P	S	V	Y	b	f	n
12	B	E	H	K	N	Q	S	V	Y	b	f	n
13	B	E	H	K	N	Q	T	V	Y	b	g	n
14	B	E	H	K	N	Q	T	W	Z	d	g	n
15	B	E	H	K	N	Q	T	W	Z	d	g	n
16	B	E	H	K	N	Q	T	W	Z	d	g	n
17	B	E	H	K	N	Q	T	W	Z	d	g	n
18	B	E	H	K	N	Q	T	W	Z	d	g	n
19	B	E	H	K	N	Q	T	W	Z	d	g	n
20	B	F	H	K	N	Q	T	W	Z	d	g	n
21	C	F	H	L	N	Q	T	W	Z	d	g	n
22	C	F	I	L	O	R	T	W	Z	d	g	n
23	C	F	I	L	O	R	T	W	Z	d	i	q
24	C	F	I	L	O	R	U	X	a	e	i	q
25	C	F	I	L	O	R	U	X	a	e	i	q
26	C	F	I	L	O	R	U	X	a	e	i	q
27	C	F	ï	L	O	R	U	X	a	e	i	q
28	C	F	I	L	O	R	U	X	a	e	i	q
29	C	-	I	L	O	R	U	X	a	e	i	q
30	C	-	I	L	O	R	U	X	a	e	i	q
31	D	–	I	-	O	-	U	X	-	e	-	q

Row labels down the left side: D A Y   O F   M O N T H

MOON ZODIAC

Moon Age Day	0	1	2	3	4	5	6	7	8	9	10	11	12	13
A	Ca	Aq	Aq	Aq	Pi	Pi	Ar	Ar	Ar	Ta	Ta	Ge	Ge	Ge
B	Aq	Aq	Aq	Pi	Pi	Ar	Ar	Ar	Ta	Ta	Ge	Ge	Ge	Cn
C	Aq	Aq	Pi	Pi	Ar	Ar	Ar	Ta	Ta	Ge	Ge	Ge	Cn	Cn
D	Aq	Pi	Pi	Pi	Ar	Ar	Ta	Ta	Ta	Ge	Ge	Cn	Cn	Le
E	Pi	Pi	Pi	Ar	Ar	Ta	Ta	Ta	Ge	Ge	Cn	Cn	Cn	Le
F	Pi	Pi	Ar	Ar	Ar	Ta	Ta	Ge	Ge	Cn	Cn	Cn	Le	Le
G	Pi	Ar	Ar	Ar	Ta	Ta	Ge	Ge	Ge	Cn	Cn	Le	Le	Le
H	Ar	Ar	Ar	Ta	Ta	Ge	Ge	Ge	Cn	Cn	Le	Le	Le	Vi
I	Ar	Ar	Ta	Ta	Ge	Ge	Ge	Cn	Cn	Cn	Le	Le	Vi	Vi
J	Ar	Ta	Ta	Ta	Ge	Ge	Cn	Cn	Cn	Le	Le	Vi	Vi	Vi
K	Ta	Ta	Ta	Ge	Ge	Cn	Cn	Cn	Le	Le	Vi	Vi	Vi	Li
L	Ta	Ta	Ge	Ge	Ge	Cn	Cn	Le	Le	Vi	Vi	Vi	Li	Li
M	Ta	Ge	Ge	Ge	Cn	Cn	Le	Le	Le	Vi	Vi	Li	Li	Li
N	Ge	Ge	Ge	Cn	Cn	Le	Le	Le	Vi	Vi	Li	Li	Li	Sc
O	Ge	Ge	Cn	Cn	Cn	Le	Le	Vi	Vi	Li	Li	Sc	Sc	Sc
P	Ge	Cn	Cn	Cn	Le	Le	Vi	Vi	Vi	Li	Li	Sc	Sc	Sc
Q	Cn	Cn	Cn	Le	Le	Vi	Vi	Li	Li	Sc	Sc	Sc	Sa	Sa
R	Cn	Cn	Le	Le	Le	Vi	Vi	Li	Li	Li	Sc	Sc	Sa	Sa
S	Cn	Le	Le	Le	Vi	Vi	Li	Li	Li	Sc	Sc	Sa	Sa	Sa
T	Le	Le	Le	Vi	Vi	Li	Li	Li	Sc	Sc	Sa	Sa	Sa	Ca
U	Le	Le	Vi	Vi	Li	Li	Li	Sc	Sc	Sa	Sa	Ca	Ca	Ca
V	Le	Vi	Vi	Vi	Li	Li	Sc	Sc	Sc	Sa	Sa	Ca	Ca	Ca
W	Le	Vi	Vi	Li	Li	Sc	Sc	Sa	Sa	Sa	Ca	Ca	Aq	Aq
X	Vi	Vi	Li	Li	Li	Sc	Sc	Sa	Sa	Sa	Ca	Ca	Aq	Aq
Y	Vi	Li	Li	Li	Sc	Sc	Sa	Sa	Sa	Ca	Ca	Aq	Aq	Aq
Z	Li	Li	Li	Sc	Sc	Sc	Sa	Sa	Ca	Ca	Ca	Aq	Aq	Pi
a	Li	Li	Li	Sc	Sc	Sa	Sa	Sa	Ca	Ca	Aq	Aq	Pi	Pi
b	Li	Li	Sc	Sc	Sa	Sa	Ca	Ca	Ca	Aq	Aq	Pi	Pi	Ar
d	Li	Sc	Sc	Sc	Sa	Sa	Ca	Ca	Ca	Aq	Aq	Pi	Pi	Pi
e	Sc	Sc	Sc	Sa	Sa	Ca	Ca	Aq	Aq	Aq	Pi	Pi	Ar	Ar
f	Sc	Sc	Sa	Sa	Ca	Ca	Aq	Aq	Pi	Pi	Ar	Ar	Ta	Ta
g	Sc	Sa	Sa	Ca	Ca	Aq	Aq	Pi	Pi	Pi	Ar	Ar	Ta	Ta
i	Sa	Sa	Ca	Ca	Ca	Aq	Aq	Pi	Pi	Ar	Ar	Ta	Ta	Ge
m	Sa	Sa	Ca	Ca	Aq	Aq	Aq	Pi	Pi	Ar	Ar	Ta	Ta	Ge
n	Sa	Ca	Ca	Aq	Aq	Pi	Pi	Ar	Ar	Ta	Ta	Ta	Ge	Ge
q	Ca	Ca	Aq	Aq	Pi	Pi	Ar	Ar	Ar	Ta	Ta	Ge	Ge	Ge

LETTER

Ar = Aries Ta = Taurus Ge = Gemini Cn = Cancer Le = Leo
Aq = Aquarius

SIGN TABLE 2

14	15	16	17	18	19	20	21	22	23	24	25	26	27	28	29
Cn	Cn	Le	Le	Le	Vi	Vi	Li	Li	Li	Sc	Sc	Sa	Sa	Sa	Ca
Cn	Le	Le	Le	Vi	Vi	Li	Li	Li	Sc	Sc	Sa	Sa	Sa	Ca	Ca
Le	Le	Le	Vi	Vi	Vi	Li	Li	Sc	Sc	Sc	Sa	Sa	Ca	Ca	Ca
Le	Le	Vi	Vi	Vi	Li	Li	Sc	Sc	Sc	Sa	Sa	Ca	Ca	Aq	Aq
Le	Vi	Vi	Vi	Li	Li	Sc	Sc	Sc	Sa	Sa	Ca	Ca	Aq	Aq	Aq
Vi	Vi	Vi	Li	Li	Li	Sc	Sc	Sa	Sa	Sa	Ca	Ca	Aq	Aq	Aq
VI	Vi	Li	Li	Li	Sc	Sc	Sa	Sa	Sa	Ca	Ca	Aq	Aq	Aq	Pi
VI	Li	Li	Li	Sc	Sc	Sa	Sa	Sa	Ca	Ca	Aq	Aq	Aq	Pi	Pi
Li	Li	Li	Sc	Sc	Sc	Sa	Sa	Ca	Ca	Ca	Aq	Aq	Pi	Pi	Pi
Li	Li	Sc	Sc	Sc	Sa	Sa	Ca	Ca	Ca	Aq	Aq	Pi	Pi	Pi	Ar
Li	Sc	Sc	Sc	Sa	Sa	Ca	Ca	Ca	Aq	Aq	Pi	Pi	Pi	Ar	Ar
Li	Sc	Sc	Sa	Sa	Sa	Ca	Ca	Aq	Aq	Aq	Pi	Pi	Ar	Ar	Ar
Sc	Sc	Sa	Sa	Sa	Ca	Ca	Aq	Aq	Aq	Pi	Pi	Ar	Ar	Ar	Ta
Sc	Sa	Sa	Sa	Ca	Ca	Aq	Aq	Aq	Pi	Pi	Ar	Ar	Ar	Ta	Ta
Sa	Sa	Sa	Ca	Ca	Ca	Aq	Aq	Pi	Pi	Pi	Ar	Ar	Ta	Ta	Ta
Sa	Sa	Ca	Ca	Ca	Aq	Aq	Pi	Pi	Pi	Ar	Ar	Ta	Ta	Ta	Ge
Sa	Ca	Ca	Ca	Aq	Aq	Pi	Pi	Pi	Ar	Ar	Ta	Ta	Ta	Ge	Ge
Sa	Ca	Ca	Aq	Aq	Aq	Pi	Pi	Ar	Ar	Ar	Ta	Ta	Ge	Ge	Ge
Ca	Ca	Aq	Aq	Aq	Pi	Pi	Ar	Ar	Ar	Ta	Ta	Ge	Ge	Ge	Cn
Ca	Aq	Aq	Aq	Pi	Pi	Ar	Ar	Ar	Ta	Ta	Ge	Ge	Ge	Cn	Cn
Aq	Aq	Aq	Pi	Pi	Pi	Ar	Ar	Ta	Ta	Ta	Ge	Ge	Cn	Cn	Cn
Aq	Aq	Pi	Pi	Pi	Ar	Ar	Ta	Ta	Ta	Ge	Ge	Cn	Cn	Cn	Le
Pi	Pi	Pi	Pi	Ar	Ar	Ta	Ta	Ta	Ge	Ge	Cn	Cn	Cn	Le	Le
Pi	Pi	Pi	Ar	Ar	Ar	Ta	Ta	Ge	Ge	Ge	Cn	Cn	Le	Le	Le
Pi	Pi	Ar	Ar	Ar	Ta	Ta	Ge	Ge	Ge	Cn	Cn	Le	Le	Le	Vi
Pi	Pi	Ar	Ar	Ar	Ta	Ta	Ge	Ge	Ge	Cn	Cn	Le	Le	Le	Vi
Ar	Ar	Ar	Ar	Ta	Ta	Ge	Ge	Ge	Cn	Cn	Cn	Le	Le	Vi	Vi
Ar	Ar	Ar	Ta	Ta	Ta	Ge	Ge	Cn	Cn	Cn	Le	Le	Vi	Vi	Vi
Ar	Ar	Ta	Ta	Ge	Ge	Ge	Cn	Cn	Cn	Le	Le	Vi	Vi	Vi	Li
Ta	Ta	Ta	Ge	Ge	Ge	Cn	Cn	Cn	Le	Le	Le	Vi	Vi	Li	Li
Ge	Ta	Ge	Ge	Ge	Cn	Cn	Cn	Le	Le	Le	Vi	Vi	Li	Li	Li
Ge	Ta	Ge	Ge	Cn	Cn	Cn	Le	Le	Le	Vi	Vi	Li	Li	Li	Sc
Ge	Ge	Ge	Cn	Cn	Cn	Le	Le	Vi	Vi	Vi	Li	Li	Sc	Sc	Sc
Ge	Ge	Cn	Cn	Cn	Le	Le	Le	Vi	Vi	Vi	Li	Li	Sc	Sc	Sa
Cn	Ge	Cn	Cn	Le	Le	Le	Vi	Vi	Vi	Li	Li	Sc	Sc	Sc	Sa
Cn	Cn	Cn	Le	Le	Le	Vi	Vi	Li	Li	Li	Sc	Sc	Sa	Sa	Sa

Vi = Virgo Li = Libra Sc = Scorpio Sa = Sagittarius Ca = Capricorn Pi = Pisces

MOON SIGNS

MOON IN ARIES

You have a strong imagination and a desire to do things in your own way. Showing no lack of courage you can forge your own path through life with great determination.

Originality is one of your most important attributes, you are seldom stuck for an idea though your mind is very changeable and more attention might be given over to one job at once. Few have the ability to order you around and you can be quite quick tempered. A calm and relaxed attitude is difficult for you to adopt but because you put tremendous pressure on your nervous system it is vitally important for you to forget about the cut and thrust of life from time to time. It would be fair to say that you rarely get the rest that you both need and deserve and becaue of this there is a chance that your health could break down from time to time.

Emotionally speaking you can be a bit of a mess if you don't talk to the folks that you are closest to and work out how you really feel about things. Once you discover that there are people willing to help you there is suddenly less necessity for trying to tackle everything yourself.

MOON IN TAURUS

The Moon in Taurus at the time you were born gives you a courteous and friendly manner that is likely to assure you of many friends.

The good things in life mean a great deal to you for Taurus is an Earth sign and delights in experiences that please the senses. This probably makes you a lover of good food and drink and might also mean that you have to spend time on the bathroom scales balancing the delight of a healthy appetite with that of looking good which is equally important to you.

Emotionally you are fairly stable and once you have opted for a set of standards you are inclined to stick to them because Taurus is a Fixed sign and doesn't respond particularly well to change. Intuition also plays an important part in your life.

MOON IN GEMINI

The Moon in the sign of Gemini gives a warm-hearted character, full of sympathy and usually ready to help those in difficulty. In some matters you are very reserved, whilst at other
times you are articulate and chatty: this is part of the paradox
of Gemini which always brings duplicity to the nature. The
knowledge you possess of local and national affairs is very
good, this strengthens and enlivens your intellect making you
good company and endowing you with many friends. Most of
the people with whom you mix have a high opinion of you and
will stand ready to leap to your defence, not that this is
generally necessary for although you are not martial by nature,
you are more than capable of defending yourself verbally.

Travel plays an important part in your life and the naturally inquisitive quality of your mind allows you to benefit greatly
from changes in scenery. The more you mix with people from
different cultures and backgrounds the greater your interest in
life becomes and intellectual stimulus is the meat and drink of
the Gemini individual.

You can gain through reading and writing as well as the cul-
tivation of artistic pursuits but you do need plenty of rest in
order to avoid fatigue.

MOON IN CANCER

Moon in Cancer at the time of birth is a most fortunate position
since the sign of Cancer is the Moon's natural home. This
means that the qualities of compassion and understanding
given by the Moon are especially enhanced in your nature and
you cope quite well with emotional pressures that would bother
others. You are friendly and sociably inclined. Domestic tasks
don't really bother you and your greatest love is likely to be for
home and family. Your surroundings are particularly important and you hate squalor and filth.

Your basic character, although at times changeable like the
Moon itself, depends upon symmetry. Little wonder then that
you are almost certain to have a love of music and poetry. Not
surprising either that you do all within your power to make
your surroundings comfortable and harmonious, not only for
yourself, but on behalf of the folk who mean so much to you.

MOON IN LEO

You are especially ambitious and self-confident. The best qualities of both the Moon and the Sign of Leo come together here to ensure that you are warm-hearted and fair, characteristics that are almost certain to show through no matter what other planetary positions your chart contains.

You certainly don't lack the ability to organise, either yourself or those around you, and you invariably rise to a position of responsibility no matter what you decide to do with your life. Perhaps it is just as well because you don't enjoy being an'also ran' and would much rather be an important part of a small organisation than a menial in a larger one.

In love you are likely to be lucky and happy provided that youput in that extra bit of effort and you can be relied upon to build comfortable home surroundings for yourself and also those for whom you feel a particular responsibility. It is likely that you will have a love of pleasure and sport and perhaps a fondness for music and literature. Life brings you many rewards, though most of them are as a direct result of the effort that you are able to put in on your own behalf. All the same you are inclined to be more lucky than average and will usually make the best of any given circumstance.

MOON IN VIRGO

This position of the Moon endows you with good mental abilities and a keen receptive memory. By nature you are probably quite reserved, nevertheless you have many friends, especially of the opposite sex, and you gain a great deal as a result of these associations. Marital relationships need to be discussed carefully and kept as harmonious as possible because personal attachments can be something of a problem to you if sufficient attention is not given to the way you handle them.

You are not ostentatious or pretentious, two characteristics that are sure to improve your popularity. Talented and persevering you possess artistic qualities and are a good homemaker. Earning your honours through genuine merit you can work long and hard towards your objectives but probably show very little pride in your genuine achievements. Many short journeys will be undertaken in your life.

MOON IN LIBRA

With the Moon in Libra you have a popular nature and don't find it particularly difficult to make friends. Most folk like you, probably more than you think, and all get-together's would be more fun with you present. Libra, for all its good points, is not the most stable of astrological signs and as a result your emotions can prove to be a little unstable too. Although the Moon in Libra is generally said to be good for love and marriage, the position of the Sun, and also the Rising Sign, in your own birth chart will have a greater than usual bearing on your emotional and loving qualities.

You cannot live your life in isolation and must rely on other people, who are likely to play an important part in your decision making. Cooperation is crucial for you because Libra represents the 'balance' of life that can only be achieved through harmonious relationships. An offshoot of this fact is that you do not enjoy being disliked and, like all Librans are friendly to practically everybody.

Conformity is not always easy for you, because Libra is an Air sign and likes to go its own way.

MOON IN SCORPIO

Some people might call you a little pushy, in fact all you really want to do is live your life to the full, and to protect yourself and your family from the pressures of life that you recognise all too readily. You should avoid giving the impression of being sarcastic or too impulsive, at the same time using your energies wisely and in a constructive manner.

Nobody could doubt your courage which is great, and you invariably achieve what you set out to do, by force of personality as well as by the effort that you are able to put in. You are fond of mystery and are probably quite perceptive as to the outcome of situations and events.

Problems can arise in your relationships with members of the opposite sex, so before you commit yourself emotionally it is very important to examine your motives carefully and ensure that the little demon, jealousy, always a problem with Scorpio positions, does not cloud your judgement in love matches. You need to travel and can make gains as a result.

MOON IN SAGITTARIUS

The Moon is Sagittarius helps to make you a generous individual with humanitarian qualities and a kind heart. Restlessness may be an endemic part of your character for your mind is seldom still. Perhaps because of this you have an overwhelming need for change that could lead you to several major moves during your adult life. You are probably a reasonably sporting sort of person and not afraid to stand your ground on the occasions when you know that you are correct in your judgement. What you have to say goes right to the heart of the matter and your intuition is very good.

At work you are quick and efficient in whatever you choose to do, and because you are versatile you make an ideal employee. Ideally you need work that is intellectually demanding because you are no drudge and would not enjoy tedious routines. In relationships you anger quickly if faced with stupidity or deception, though you are just as quick to forgive and forget. Emotionally there are times when you allow your heart to rule your head.

MOON IN CAPRICORN

Born with the Moon in Capricorn, you are popular and may come into the public eye in one way or another. Your administrative ability is good and you are a capable worker. The watery Moon is not entirely at home in the Earth sign of Capricorn and as a result difficulties can be experienced, especially in the early years of life. Some initial lack of creative ability and indecision has to be overcome before the true qualities of patience and perseverance inherent in Capricorn can show through.

If caution is exercised in financial affairs you can accumulate wealth with the passing of time but you will always have to be careful about forming any partnerships because you are open to deception more than most. Under such circumstances you would be well-advised to gain professional advice before committing yourself. Many people with the Moon in Capricorn take a healthy interest in social or welfare work. The organisational skills that you have, together with a genuine sympathy for others, means that you are suited to this kind of career.

MOON IN AQUARIUS

With the Moon in Aquarius you are an active and agreeable person with a friendly easy going sort of nature. Being sympathetic to the needs of other people you flourish best in an easy going atmosphere. You are broad-minded, just, and open to suggestion, though as with all faces of Aquarius the Moon here brings an unconventional quality that not everyone would find easy to understand.

You have a liking for anything strange and curious as well a fascination for old articles and places. Journeys to such locations would suit you doubly because you love to travel and can gain a great deal from the trips that you make. Political, scientific and educational work might all be of interest to you and you would gain from a career in some new and exciting branch of science or technology.

Money-wise, you make gains through innovation as much as by concentration and it isn't unusual to find lunar Aquarians tackling more than one job at the same time. In love you are honest and kind.

MOON IN PISCES

This position assures you of a kind sympathetic nature, somewhat retiring at times but always taking account of others and doing your best to help them. As with all planets in Pisces there is bound to be some misfortune on the way through life. In particular relationships of a personal nature can be problematic and often through no real fault of your own. Inevitably though suffering brings a better understanding, both of yourself and of the world around you. With a fondness for travel you appreciate beauty and harmony wherever you encounter them and hate disorder and strife.

You are probably very fond of literature and could make a good writer or speaker yourself. The imagination that you possess can be readily translated into creativity and you might come across as an incurable romantic. Being naturally receptive your intuition is strong, in many cases verging on a mediumistic quality that sets you apart from the world. You might not be rich in hard cash terms and yet the gifts that you possess and display, when used properly, are worth more than gold.

THE ASTRAL DIARY

How the diagrams work

Through the *picture diagrams* in the Astral Diary I want to help you to plot your year. With them you can see where the positive and negative aspects will be found each month. To make the most of them all you have to do is remember where and when!

Let me show you how they work . . .

THE MONTH AT A GLANCE

Just as there are twelve separate Zodiac Signs, so Astrologers believe that each sign has twelve separate aspects to life. Each of the twelve segments relates to a different personal aspect. I number and list them all every month as a key so that their meanings are always clear.

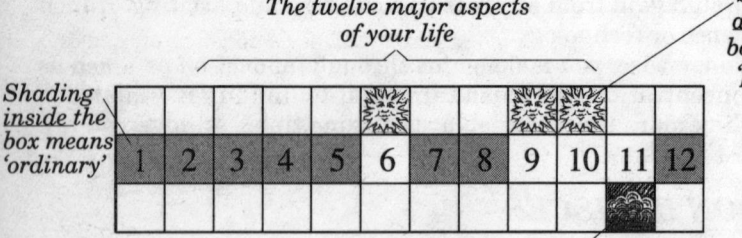

The twelve major aspects of your life

Symbols above the box means 'positive'

Shading inside the box means 'ordinary'

Symbol below the box means 'negative'

I have designed this chart to show you how and when these twelve different aspects are being influenced throughout the year. When the number rests comfortably in its shaded box, nothing out of the ordinary is to be expected. However, when a box turns white, then you should expect influences to become active in this area of your life. Where the influence is positive I have raised a smiling sun above its number. Where it is a negative, I hang a little rain cloud beneath it.

YOUR ENERGY RHYTHM CHART

On the opposite page is a picture diagram in which I am linking your zodiac group to the rhythm of the moon. In doing this I have calculated when you will be gaining strength from its influence and equally when you may be weakened by it.

If you think of yourself as being like the tides of the ocean then you may understand how your own energies must rise and fall too. And if you understand how it works and when it is working, then you can better organise your activities to achieve more and get things done more easily.

YOUR ENERGY-RHYTHM CHART

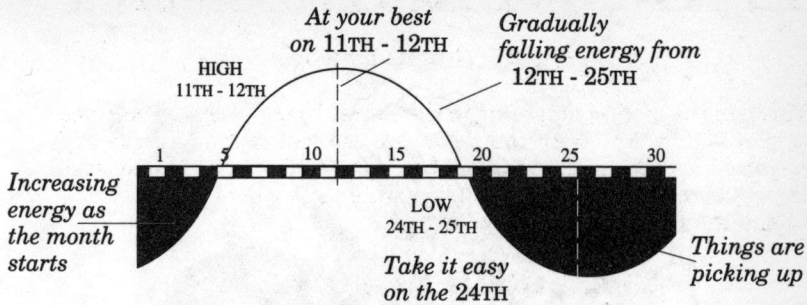

At your best on 11TH - 12TH

HIGH 11TH - 12TH

Gradually falling energy from 12TH - 25TH

Increasing energy as the month starts

LOW 24TH - 25TH

Take it easy on the 24TH

Things are picking up

MOVING PICTURE SCREEN
Measured every week

LOVE, LUCK, MONEY & VITALITY

I hope that the diagram below offers more than a little fun. It is very easy to use. The bars move across the scale to give you some idea of the strength of opportunities open to you in each of the four areas. If LOVE stands at plus 4, then get out and put yourself about, because in terms of romance, things should be going your way. When the bar moves backwards then the opportunities are weakening and when it enters the negative scale, then romance should not be at the top of your list.

Not a good week for money

← NEGATIVE TREND

POSITIVE TREND →

Love at +4 promises a romantic week

	-5	-4	-3	-2	-1		+1	+2	+3	+4	+5
LOVE											
MONEY											
LUCK											
VITALITY											

Below average for vitality

And your luck in general is good

And Finally:

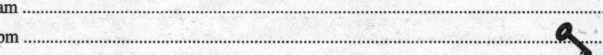

am ....

pm ....

The two lines that are left blank in each daily entry of the Astral Diary are for your own personal use. You may find them ideal for keeping a check on birthdays or appointments, though it could be an idea to make notes from the astrological trends and diagrams a few weeks in advance. Some of the lines carry a key, as above. These days are important because they indicate the working of 'astrological cycles' in your life. The key readings show how best you can act, react or simply work within them for greater success.

1995

YOUR MONTH AT A GLANCE

The twelve numbered boxes represent the important areas in your life.
The key to the numbers you will find beneath the panel. A Sun above
the number indicates that opportunities are around. A Cloud below
the number, that you should be a bit defensive. Nothing above or
below and life will be pretty ordinary.

1	2	3	4	5	6 ☀	7	8 ☀	9	10 ☀	11	12

(Clouds below boxes 4 and 5)

KEY

1 Strength of Personality	7 One to One Relationships
2 Personal Finance	8 Questioning, Thinking & Deciding
3 Useful Information Gathering	9 External Influences / Education
4 Domestic Affairs	10 Career Aspirations
5 Pleasure & Romance	11 Teamwork Activities
6 Effective Work & Health	12 Unconscious Impulses

OCTOBER HIGHS AND LOWS

Here, I show how the rhythm of the Moon will affect you this month.
Like the tide, your energies and abilities will rise and fall with its pattern. When it is above the date line, go-for-it. When it is below the
line you should be resting.

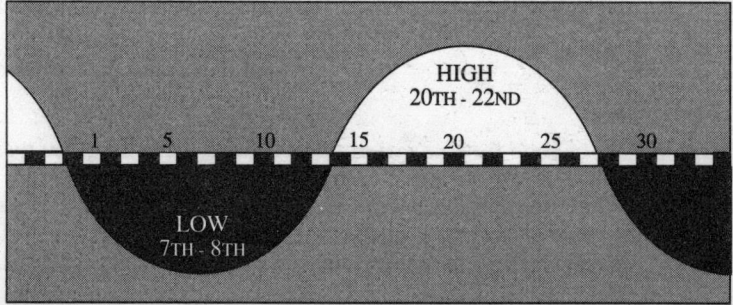

2 MONDAY
Moon Age Day 8 • Moon Sign Capricorn

am ....

pm ....

The strength of your ego begins to show today as you start to put your own ideas into practice. Nobody is likely to be in a position to argue with you, mainly because you won't allow them the chance. At work routines begin to take on a more interesting feel and you manage to keep yourself active most of the time.

3 TUESDAY
Moon Age Day 9 • Moon Sign Capricorn

am ....

pm ....

Discussions tend to falter today, not because you are unwilling to pursue them, but on account of your inability to see things in quite the constructive way that you normally might. A brave Virgoan is in evidence and there is reason to believe that you will tackle topics later that you may have been avoiding.

4 WEDNESDAY
Moon Age Day 10 • Moon Sign Aquarius

am ....

pm ....

Your romantic partner may appear to be giving you the runaroud at the moment, which is a situation you really have no choice but to deal with as best you can. Confidence appears to be at an all time low, though it shouldn't be long until you find ways and means to pull yourself together and get on with everyday life.

5 THURSDAY
Moon Age Day 11 • Moon Sign Aquarius

am ....

pm ....

Make plenty of time for relaxation and for doing anything you want that relates specifically to you. With plenty of zest for the prospect of life, though without the apparent energy to do much about it, you might find yourself stuck between a rock and a hard place. Not a dynamic day, but useful to you all the same.

6 FRIDAY

Moon Age Day 12 ‹ Moon Sign Pisces

am ....

pm ....

It is possible that someone in your vicinity may be able to make the sort of progress that you personally find impossible for now. If this turns out to be the case it would be sensible to allow them to have their head for a while, as you sit back and enjoy what benefits accrue from their efforts. Stick to what you know.

7 SATURDAY

Moon Age Day 13 ‹ Moon Sign Pisces

am ....

pm ....

Although still not at the luckiest part of the month, there are things that are working to your advantage, not least of all in terms of your personal life. Confidence looks as though it is beginning to grow again and someone in your vicinity has plenty to say for themselves, probably much to your satisfaction.

8 SUNDAY

Moon Age Day 14 ‹ Moon Sign Aries

am ....

pm ....

All unfinished business now becomes more of a possibility and you are able to give yourself a pat on the back for getting through masses of work, and in half the usual time. You may have to get your head round certain facts that you don't care for the look of, but in the days ahead can still come out as the winner.

	← *NEGATIVE TREND*							*POSITIVE TREND* →			
-5	-4	-3	-2	-1		+1	+2	+3	+4	+5
					LOVE					
					MONEY					
					LUCK					
					VITALITY					

9 MONDAY

Moon Age Day 15 ‹ Moon Sign Aries

am ....

pm ....

The day is hectic, though that does not mean that it fails to be positive in any way. A real coup at work seems possible, with those of influence and power now more willing than ever to see your point of view and to follow it whenever necessary. Old events now tend to be replayed in your mind, in a different order.

10 TUESDAY

Moon Age Day 16 ‹ Moon Sign Taurus

am ....

pm ....

You are able to bring out the best in others, and by so doing manage to feather your own nest on the way. Be brave and certain that what you want from life is right because your intuition is strong and there is plenty working in your favour. Some good days lie ahead of you, in which you can be a genuine individual.

11 WEDNESDAY

Moon Age Day 17 ‹ Moon Sign Taurus

am ....

pm ....

You ought to be able to satisfy your own curiosity about a number of things now. The attitudes of people in your vicinity are about to change in your favour, which is one of the reasons why you are altering slightly yourself. Powers of recall are good and you can use the past as a yardstick for judging the future.

12 THURSDAY

Moon Age Day 18 ‹ Moon Sign Taurus

am ....

pm ....

Although there is little scope for expansion, or for broadening your mind as much as you might wish to, there is always the chance that things turn out differently than you imagined. With greater perseverance than seems to be possible at first, you will be amazed at just how much you can actually get done.

13 FRIDAY   *Moon Age Day 19 ‹ Moon Sign Gemini*

am ....

pm ....

Even though it is Friday the thirteenth, there is no reason at all why this day should turn out to be anything other than positive. Carefully and skilfully you can avoid creating any sort of problem for yourself and could even find that you are making financial progress before the day is out.

14 SATURDAY   *Moon Age Day 20 ‹ Moon Sign Gemini*

am ....

pm ....

You are likely to be distracted from your chosen path in life, mainly because of the problems that other people bring in. Applying yourself diligently to the task in hand is interesting and offers possibilities that, at this point in time, you probably have not thought about. Confidence is growing again.

15 SUNDAY   *Moon Age Day 21 ‹ Moon Sign Cancer*

am ....

pm ....

Discussions are made more interesting and informed debate becomes more possible now, so that you find yourself in a position to move forward in your life slowly and progressively. The actions of others may not be all that easy to predict, though that does not mean that they are working against your best interests.

← NEGATIVE TREND						POSITIVE TREND →				
-5	-4	-3	-2	-1		+1	+2	+3	+4	+5
					LOVE					
					MONEY					
					LUCK					
					VITALITY					

16 MONDAY

Moon Age Day 22 ‹ Moon Sign Cancer

am ....

pm ....

An unexpected visitor from far away is a possibility now, as is the chance for you to do what you want in terms of your own travel arrangements. Organise the practical elements of life in any way that you wish, and keep an open mind about the way that personal relationships seem to be working out for the moment.

17 TUESDAY

Moon Age Day 23 ‹ Moon Sign Cancer

am ....

pm ....

You do tend to lack personal influence right now, which is something that you have to deal with in an hour by hour sense. Feeling that you are not entirely in charge of your own life is something that you find difficult to come to terms with, though that does not mean that the situation is an impossibility.

18 WEDNESDAY

Moon Age Day 24 ‹ Moon Sign Leo

am ....

pm ....

Opportunities to positively influence the financial side of your life come from all sorts of directions today, and indeed for several more to come. A new phase opens up in your life and one that is far more dynamic in prospect than almost anything that has gone before. Keep out of your partner's hair for a while.

19 THURSDAY

Moon Age Day 25 ‹ Moon Sign Leo

am ....

pm ....

Short journeys bring significant rewards into your life as a whole, as do any form of business meeting that you have looked at and planned carefully. You must be aware that there is no mileage in letting off steam in public about issues that would be best left entirely alone. Be determined in professional matters.

20 FRIDAY
Moon Age Day 26 ‹ Moon Sign Virgo

am ....

pm ....

The moon assists, and along comes a period when you can genuinely have most things your own way. There are situations about that you can turn to your own advantage, not least of all in terms of relationships, which look as though they are going to be easier to deal with for a while. People are more generous towards you.

21 SATURDAY
Moon Age Day 27 ‹ Moon Sign Virgo

am ....

pm ....

Whatever it is that you decide to put your mind to at present, there is more than a little chance that it turns itself to your advantage. Friends and colleagues are highly motivated in the direction of helping you to do what you would wish, whilst there are gains to be made, the nature of which you could only guess at.

22 SUNDAY
Moon Age Day 28 ‹ Moon Sign Virgo

am ....

pm ....

Facing financial obligations is not going to be something that you really want to look at all that closely just for now. The reaction of those around you tends to be rather different than you may expect and situations generally do not turn out quite as you might have hoped. Be willing to let others lend a hand.

← *NEGATIVE TREND*   *POSITIVE TREND* →

-5	-4	-3	-2	-1			+1	+2	+3	+4	+5
					LOVE						
					MONEY						
					LUCK						
					VITALITY						

23 MONDAY
Moon Age Day 0 ‹ Moon Sign Libra

am ....

pm ....

An air of irritation exists in the sphere of personal relationships, and it's something that you have to be aware of if you are going to prevent it from having too important a part to play in your life. A continued reliance on the favours coming from the direction of friends is something that you won't want.

24 TUESDAY
Moon Age Day 1 ‹ Moon Sign Libra

am ....

pm ....

As the sun enters your solar third house, so you discover that you have about a month in front of you when obtaining information vital to your life becomes that much easier. You can easily handle several different situations at the same time, without any undue stress being placed upon you while you do it.

25 WEDNESDAY
Moon Age Day 2 ‹ Moon Sign Scorpio

am ....

pm ....

Discussions of an important nature are now taking place, and you won't want to miss out on any of them. The pace of your everyday life is slowing, allowing greater freedom to please yourself in out of work activities and also providing you with the chance to build new and interesting patterns into your life.

26 THURSDAY
Moon Age Day 3 ‹ Moon Sign Scorpio

am ....

pm ....

You feel a definite need for familiar places and faces, as you withdraw into yourself more than might usually be the case, even for your sign. Confrontation is clearly something that you would want to avoid, even though it is possible that other people put you in a position that makes it difficult for you to do so.

27 FRIDAY   *Moon Age Day 4 ‹ Moon Sign Sagittarius*

am ....

pm ....

Don't be in too much of a hurry to get things done, or to change things in your life before you have had the time to think about them fully. Significant changes are at hand, but many of them take a while to come into play. Meanwhile it can be rather frustrating to carry on as if everything was quite normal.

28 SATURDAY   *Moon Age Day 5 ‹ Moon Sign Sagittarius*

am ....

pm ....

Overlooking important details is something that you want to avoid right now, so it is very important to keep your eye firmly on the future. Later, a romantic situation becomes possible and there are new options to be considered in other spheres of your life too. Don't take any action that you know to be provocative.

29 SUNDAY   *Moon Age Day 6 ‹ Moon Sign Capricorn*

am ....

pm ....

Allowing people to talk you out of things that you want to do would not be either wise or sensible at present. The days ahead are certainly not ones in which you will want to be creeping about or hiding your true potential and there is plenty for you to get your teeth into now your level of energy is so high.

← NEGATIVE TREND							POSITIVE TREND →			
-5	-4	-3	-2	-1		+1	+2	+3	+4	+5
					LOVE					
					MONEY					
					LUCK					
					VITALITY					

30 MONDAY
Moon Age Day 7 ‹ Moon Sign Capricorn

am ....

pm ....

Unfortunately, some of your less favourable trends are on display at present and you should certainly do your best to make certain that you are willing to give and take. The ability of Virgo subjects to be stubborn is quite well known and that is especially relevant under prevailing circumstances.

31 TUESDAY
Moon Age Day 8 ‹ Moon Sign Aquarius

am ....

pm ....

The need to put across your opinions in a positive and definite manner is something that you will be thinking about a great deal just at the moment. Be aware that you need a sense of continuity in your life and that you can only really achieve it by being willing to allow things to settle in a day to day sense.

1 WEDNESDAY
Moon Age Day 9 ‹ Moon Sign Aquarius

am ....

pm ....

Try not to become bored with too many tedious and boring routines, all of which you know have to be done but none of which you are particularly looking forward to right now. Where you can defer things until a later date it might be sensible to do so, if only because you need more space to do exactly what pleases you.

2 THURSDAY
Moon Age Day 10 ‹ Moon Sign Pisces

am ....

pm ....

You can run out of steam all too easily at present, and since it is the present position of the moon that is responsible for this situation, there is not much that you can do about it except settle back and wait for the situation to clear a little. Beware, it is all too easy to make some awkward mistakes.

3 FRIDAY

Moon Age Day 11 ‹ Moon Sign Pisces

am ....

pm ....

Setbacks are still around, though probably not for the whole day. Actions are speaking louder than words in most situations, so that you have great incentive to do whatever takes your fancy in a practical sense, even if you do not particularly want to talk about them all the time. Allow for periods of quietness.

4 SATURDAY

Moon Age Day 12 ‹ Moon Sign Aries

am ....

pm ....

The domestic atmosphere should be especially pleasant for now, and this fact allows you to look ahead in a house and home sense more effectively than has been the case for quite some time. Controlling situations that could prove to be stressful is something that you excel at during the weekend and beyond.

5 SUNDAY

Moon Age Day 13 ‹ Moon Sign Aries

am ....

pm ....

You can put the finishing touches to all manner of projects that have been on the go for a while now. You avoid social issues just as much as you can and will opt, instead, for getting on with the everyday work that has to be done around your home. Not everyone is equally helpful in their efforts on your behalf.

← *NEGATIVE TREND*   *POSITIVE TREND* →

-5	-4	-3	-2	-1		+1	+2	+3	+4	+5
					LOVE					
					MONEY					
					LUCK					
					VITALITY					

1995

YOUR MONTH AT A GLANCE

The twelve numbered boxes represent the important areas in your life.
The key to the numbers you will find beneath the panel. A Sun above
the number indicates that opportunities are around. A Cloud below
the number, that you should be a bit defensive. Nothing above or
below and life will be pretty ordinary.

1	2	3	4	5	6	7	8	9	10	11	12

KEY

1 Strength of Personality
2 Personal Finance
3 Useful Information Gathering
4 Domestic Affairs
5 Pleasure & Romance
6 Effective Work & Health

7 One to One Relationships
8 Questioning, Thinking & Deciding
9 External Influences / Education
10 Career Aspirations
11 Teamwork Activities
12 Unconscious Impulses

NOVEMBER HIGHS AND LOWS

Here, I show how the rhythm of the Moon will affect you this month.
Like the tide, your energies and abilities will rise and fall with its pattern. When it is above the date line, go-for-it. When it is below the
line you should be resting.

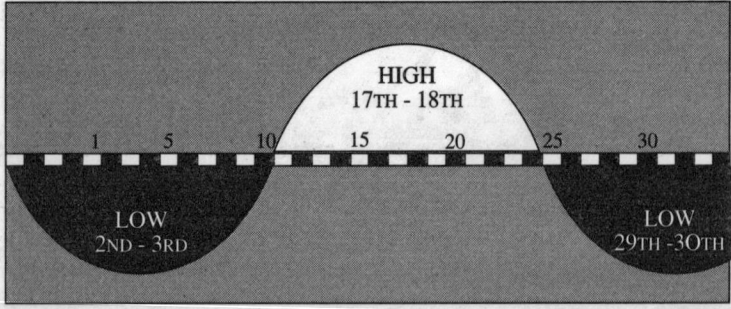

6 MONDAY
Moon Age Day 14 • Moon Sign Aries

am ....

pm ....

Mundane responsiblities can get in the way of your progress, which would be a pity at a time when most things should be going very well. Try to ring the changes whenever you can and avoid allowing yourself to be tied down too much by details that probably don't really matter all that much in the long-run.

7 TUESDAY
Moon Age Day 15 • Moon Sign Taurus

am ....

pm ....

It looks as though family members will not behave in quite the way you would wish them to, at least not for the moment. Personalities abound in your life, especially close to home where there is the possibility of new friendships emerging and alternative interests playing a part in your daily routines.

8 WEDNESDAY
Moon Age Day 16 • Moon Sign Taurus

am ....

pm ....

Excitement begins to mount as you start to realise that almost anything is possible. With a greater sense of urgency, together with plenty of incentive to get ahead, you put your best foot forward in almost everything that you attempt. Even where there is deadline to meet, you rise wonderfully to the challenge.

9 THURSDAY
Moon Age Day 17 • Moon Sign Gemini

am ....

pm ....

The high profile continues, thanks to some especially helpful aspects in your chart. Few people could deflect you from whatever path it is you choose to take in life. Reassurance is necessary from others when you find yourself doing things that have not been an integral part of your experience in the past.

51

10 FRIDAY
Moon Age Day 18 ‹ Moon Sign Gemini

am ....

pm ....

Family members, and loved ones generally, could be trying your patience today more than would usually be the case. If this turns out to be true, all you can really do is to be as calm about the situation as you know how to be, and not to allow it to rattle you too much. In a personal sense you are seeking freedom.

11 SATURDAY
Moon Age Day 19 ‹ Moon Sign Gemini

am ....

pm ....

Original characters and a very different sort of life are what you want to seek right now. Be bold and adventurous, though do remember that there are routines that have to be dealt with too. The weekend does offer some scope for change, even though it could be quite a while before it really begins to show.

12 SUNDAY
Moon Age Day 20 ‹ Moon Sign Cancer

am ....

pm ....

Curiosity is stimulated today, and you want to know the ins and outs of almost everything that you come across. Not everyone is equally useful when it comes to deciding just how you should get on with the practical requirements of life, though as long as you are patient with yourself, the answers lie around every corner now.

← NEGATIVE TREND							POSITIVE TREND →				
-5	-4	-3	-2	-1			+1	+2	+3	+4	+5
					LOVE						
					MONEY						
					LUCK						
					VITALITY						

13 MONDAY
Moon Age Day 21 ‹ Moon Sign Cancer

am ....

pm ....

Those closest to you can seem to be especially edgy and more than a little difficult for you to deal with. Don't allow your nervous system to work overtime for now and act only after you have thought about things just as carefully as you can. Rest and relaxation are important factors in the general order of your day.

14 TUESDAY
Moon Age Day 22 ‹ Moon Sign Leo

am ....

pm ....

You need to keep to a strictly practical routine, for there are gains to be made from not allowing yourself to be stifled or held back from destinations that you recognise to be in your sight. Emotionally speaking, you are not really acting as sensibly as your might and may need the timely advice of a partner or friend.

15 WEDNESDAY
Moon Age Day 23 ‹ Moon Sign Leo

am ....

pm ....

Short trips or meetings that you have the chance to undertake at any stage this week can be turned to your distinct advantage. This is the commencement of an astrological phase that promises many more gains personally and the opportunity to find fresh fields and pastures new, even in a deeply personal sense.

16 THURSDAY
Moon Age Day 24 ‹ Moon Sign Leo

am ....

pm ....

The present position of the moon is a real confidence booster as far as you are concerned, and, taken together with other favourable trends just now, promises much in the way that you push forward for the remainder of the week and beyond. Luck is on your side and you can afford to take the odd chance now.

17 FRIDAY

Moon Age Day 25 ‹ Moon Sign Virgo

am ....

pm ....

Is it really amazing the way others gather round to help you out, or is it merely that they recognise in you the sort of person who can be of help to them, courtesy of your own present positive state? Whatever the truth of the fact, you would be unwise to fail in your recognition of what turns out to be an excellent period.

18 SATURDAY

Moon Age Day 26 ‹ Moon Sign Virgo

am ....

pm ....

There may be some risk attached to certain ventures, though of course it is necessary to take a chance once in a while. The stresses and strains of recent periods could threaten to catch up with you presently, and it is your duty to avoid the possibility by making certain that you remain on an even keel as much as possible.

19 SUNDAY

Moon Age Day 27 ‹ Moon Sign Libra

am ....

pm ....

In company you have the ability to shine out well, so much so that you are the life and soul of almost any party that is taking place around you this weekend. Creating just the right impression is something that you just cannot wait to do, and there is nobody better than a Virgo when he or she is on form.

← NEGATIVE TREND							POSITIVE TREND →			
-5	-4	-3	-2	-1		+1	+2	+3	+4	+5
					LOVE					
					MONEY					
					LUCK					
					VITALITY					

20 MONDAY

Moon Age Day 28 ‹ Moon Sign Libra

am ....

pm ....

This is an excellent day for all interests that are centred around your home, even if you know that there are duties outside that demand quite a portion of your attention. An occasional day or at least an early finish to work would allow you spend a little more time with close family members.

21 TUESDAY

Moon Age Day 29 ‹ Moon Sign Scorpio

am ....

pm ....

What you expect from others today, and what actually turns out to be the truth, could be too entirely different things, which is why you have to be particularly careful before you allow yourself to get more involved with them than you can avoid. All in all you would be well advised to keep yourself to yourself for now.

22 WEDNESDAY

Moon Age Day 0 ‹ Moon Sign Scorpio

am ....

pm ....

A new period dawns affecting your house and home, as the sun moves into your solar fourth house. Those people dear to you, and your own surroundings, are the areas of life that offer the best form of advantage in the month ahead. In most circumstances you need not look further than your own front door for help.

23 THURSDAY

Moon Age Day 1 ‹ Moon Sign Sagittarius

am ....

pm ....

There is a definite tendency towards laziness that you really cannot get over today. Why try? It might just be better to work within the possibilities and deal with your day accordingly. In any case you do yourself no favours if you decide that you are going to put yourself under masses of pressure in the hours ahead.

24 FRIDAY
Moon Age Day 2 ‹ Moon Sign Sagittarius

am ....

pm ....

You do need to occupy centre stage now, that is if you want to get ahead in the romantic and personal stakes. Offers of help to do this come from all sorts of directions, though whether or not you tend to realise the fact does remain to be seen. You can sometimes be a little deaf to what others are trying to say to you.

25 SATURDAY
Moon Age Day 3 ‹ Moon Sign Capricorn

am ....

pm ....

Make certain that loved ones and family members in general understand what it is that you are trying to say to them. Comfort and security play an important part in your thinking and you need the support that comes from feeling settled with your lot. Finances are not quite as important as they first appear.

26 SUNDAY
Moon Age Day 4 ‹ Moon Sign Capricorn

am ....

pm ....

You may find that your need to occupy centre stage takes on new proportions today. This is really no bad thing, and especially not for Virgo subjects who do not work during the weekend. You are probably further ahead with certain jobs than you expect and so can afford to slow things down for just a few hours in a practical sense.

← NEGATIVE TREND						POSITIVE TREND →				
-5	-4	-3	-2	-1		+1	+2	+3	+4	+5
					LOVE					
					MONEY					
					LUCK					
					VITALITY					

27 MONDAY

Moon Age Day 5 ‹ Moon Sign Aquarius

am ....

pm ....

There are ways in which you can improve your general lot in life, simply by making certain that you are in the right place at the right time for the next week or so. Most of the time this is an instinctive situation, though there are occasions when some careful prior thought is apt to pay quite handsome dividends later.

28 TUESDAY

Moon Age Day 6 ‹ Moon Sign Aquarius

am ....

pm ....

Loved ones have a habit of bringing up issues from the past that you would probably rather get away from if you possibly can. Where this proves to be a non-starter, you will just have to look them square in the face and deal with each event on its merits. Some friendly people cross your path a little later.

29 WEDNESDAY

Moon Age Day 7 ‹ Moon Sign Pisces

am ....

pm ....

The moon moves into a position that may not turn out to quite as useful as it could be for you, though only if you try to carry on regardless and refuse to realise that there are times when it would be better to simply allow life to go at a slower pace. Romance looks good, with a new start on offer for some of you.

30 THURSDAY

Moon Age Day 8 ‹ Moon Sign Pisces

am ....

pm ....

Hardly your luckiest day of the month, and yet carrying with it the promise of things to come that may have escaped your attention in busier and less thoughtful times. Definitely a period to be planning rather than doing, and an interlude when you will be surprised at just how attentive you can be to events.

1 FRIDAY

Moon Age Day 9 ‹ Moon Sign Pisces

am ....

pm ....

A new burst of activity in the leisure and romance areas of life puts you in the best of all possible positions as you stand on the threshold of the weekend. Don't underestimate the power of your own mind, and plan ahead carefully so that you do not find yourself with more to do that you really want during next week.

2 SATURDAY

Moon Age Day 10 ‹ Moon Sign Aries

am ....

pm ....

You can get more than you bargained for today, mainly because of your own efforts in the past, together with a new astrological phase that allows you to put your talents to the test fully. Not a time for any Virgo subject to be sitting around and waiting for possibilities.

3 SUNDAY

Moon Age Day 11 ‹ Moon Sign Aries

am ....

pm ....

You need to seek out some sort of ideal change for yourself today. and can do so by being willing to sit and watch life go by for a change. Don't be too fussy in your appraisal of the way things turn out, better by far simply to wait and see. Sometimes the greatest movement of all in life is made by simply standing still.

← NEGATIVE TREND						POSITIVE TREND →				
-5	-4	-3	-2	-1		+1	+2	+3	+4	+5
					LOVE					
					MONEY					
					LUCK					
					VITALITY					

1995
YOUR MONTH AT A GLANCE

The twelve numbered boxes represent the important areas in your life. The key to the numbers you will find beneath the panel. A Sun above the number indicates that opportunities are around. A Cloud below the number, that you should be a bit defensive. Nothing above or below and life will be pretty ordinary.

			☀	☀							
1	2	3	4	5	6	7	8	9	10	11	12
	☁										

KEY

1 Strength of Personality
2 Personal Finance
3 Useful Information Gathering
4 Domestic Affairs
5 Pleasure & Romance
6 Effective Work & Health

7 One to One Relationships
8 Questioning, Thinking & Deciding
9 External Influences / Education
10 Career Aspirations
11 Teamwork Activities
12 Unconscious Impulses

DECEMBER HIGHS AND LOWS

Here, I show how the rhythm of the Moon will affect you this month. Like the tide, your energies and abilities will rise and fall with its pattern. When it is above the date line, go-for-it. When it is below the line you should be resting.

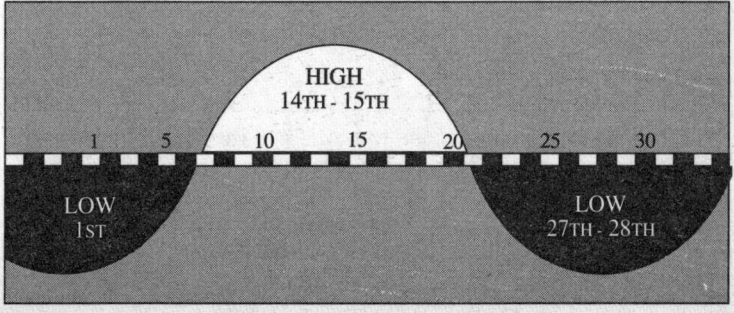

4 MONDAY
Moon Age Day 12 • Moon Sign Taurus

am ....

pm ....

Well ahead of your own personal schedule in most matters, you are surprised at just how much gets done at the start of this working week, and all because you put yourself in the right frame of mind to make the most of prevailing circumstances. Too much concentration could be as bad as too little in the end though.

5 TUESDAY
Moon Age Day 13 • Moon Sign Taurus

am ....

pm ....

You tend to be the star attraction for the moment. Why not make more out of the situation by taking other people at their word and allowing them to play a part in you life greater than would usually be the case. It is a problem of your sign that you are inclined to want to go it alone, too much for your own good sometimes.

6 WEDNESDAY
Moon Age Day 14 • Moon Sign Gemini

am ....

pm ....

It is possible that you find yourself having to find quick answers to questions that are of extreme importance. Never mind, your reactions can be like lightning when you choose and you are unlikely to be held back by anyone or anything during the middle of this week. It is possible to work hard and to relax at the same time.

7 THURSDAY
Moon Age Day 15 • Moon Sign Gemini

am ....

pm ....

Discussions with people close to home are inclined to cheer you up more than you might imagine, not only for today but during the whole of the week that lies ahead. Where you have been dreading a particular job, now is the time to realise that there can be enjoyment in almost anything you do, if it is done really well.

8 FRIDAY

Moon Age Day 16 ‹ Moon Sign Gemini

am ....

pm ....

Teamwork or activities that put you closely in touch with the world on your doorstep are of supreme importance today. It may be that you are thinking about a new sporting activity, or that you decide to bring more personal interest in your life in some other way. Romance could also play a part in your present thinking.

9 SATURDAY

Moon Age Day 17 ‹ Moon Sign Cancer

am ....

pm ....

Romance once again rears its head, and probably no matter what your age or marital status. It could be that your partner is being more attentive than would usually be the case of simply that you find the offers around you more interesting than might normally be so. Less personally speaking, don't listen to rumours.

10 SUNDAY

Moon Age Day 18 ‹ Moon Sign Cancer

am ....

pm ....

You are now too responsive to what others are saying, not exactly a good state of affairs for this December Sunday. All your plans at present need to be your own, and especially those that are geared towards the Christmas period. An active Virgoan would be best, though not one that runs around all day like a headless chicken!

← *NEGATIVE TREND*   *POSITIVE TREND* →

-5	-4	-3	-2	-1			+1	+2	+3	+4	+5
					LOVE						
					MONEY						
					LUCK						
					VITALITY						

11 MONDAY

Moon Age Day 19 ‹ Moon Sign Leo

am ....

pm ....

Look to relatives and good friends, many of whom not only have some good ideas but are willing and able to assist you in putting your own schemes into practice. There are virtues to find in even the most surprising of people, and the implication of what they tell you spread out like ripples on a pond into the futures.

12 TUESDAY

Moon Age Day 20 ‹ Moon Sign Leo

am ....

pm ....

The way that you deal with priorities reflects your general attitude to life at present, since some you are willing to deal with immediately, whilst others tend to be left on the shelf for far too long. It isn't like you as a rule to put matters to the back of your mind, though beware of the tendency to do so now.

13 WEDNESDAY

Moon Age Day 21 ‹ Moon Sign Leo

am ....

pm ....

One of the best opportunities of the month for getting ahead, for making new friends and finding that you have far more influence on the world at large than might usually appear to be the case. Money matters improve, though not of their own accord. Most of the effort you put in turns into gold, at least figuratively.

14 THURSDAY

Moon Age Day 22 ‹ Moon Sign Virgo

am ....

pm ....

Your potential for luck has rarely been more accented. All the more reason for taking the strings of your own life in your hands and for pushing forward at a great pace. Personalities who come into your life at the moment have some interesting things to tell you. Make certain that you have your ears pinned back and listen.

15 FRIDAY

Moon Age Day 23 ‹ Moon Sign Virgo

am ....

pm ....

Getting your own way is not hard. The moon still occupies a very good position for you, allowing prior planning to become a definite possibility, whilst at the same time general good luck is also on your side. Even apparent setbacks can be turned to your advantage and you have energy to spare for personal ideas.

16 SATURDAY

Moon Age Day 24 ‹ Moon Sign Libra

am ....

pm ....

Avoid overspending, which although rather strange advice so close to Christmas, is very relevant never the less. It could be that some financial burdens relate, not simply to you, but to others as well. Where such people may not be pulling their weight, it would be sensible to have a quiet word with them now and sort things out.

17 SUNDAY

Moon Age Day 25 ‹ Moon Sign Libra

am ....

pm ....

Probably a day without equal this month in terms of the way that your loved ones and even friends are likely to be treating you. Keep yourself out there in the mainstream of events and do your best to enjoy the approach of the festive season. The departure of an old friend may well mark the arrival of some important new ones.

NEGATIVE TREND								POSITIVE TREND		
-5	-4	-3	-2	-1		+1	+2	+3	+4	+5
					LOVE					
					MONEY					
					LUCK					
					VITALITY					

18 MONDAY

Moon Age Day 26 ‹ Moon Sign Libra

am ....

pm ....

Attempting to do more than is really good for you is not something that you should consider for now, though caution is necessary since such situations could build up before you have the time to realise. Take some time out to relax, even if it seems impossible to do so just for the next day or two.

19 TUESDAY

Moon Age Day 27 ‹ Moon Sign Scorpio

am ....

pm ....

There may be a conflict in your mind between serving the needs of others and doing what you know to be right for you personally. Where this turns out to be the case you will just have to do your best to fulfil both objectives, even if it looks as though you are tearing yourself in half to do so. In the end, all is well.

20 WEDNESDAY

Moon Age Day 28 ‹ Moon Sign Scorpio

am ....

pm ....

Too much restlessness is never a good thing for your sign. Some form of meditation would do you good, even just in the short-term. You always need a sense of continuity in your life, though sometimes this is difficult to establish. Blind stubborn attitudes are the ones to avoid, as loved ones may well point out.

21 THURSDAY

Moon Age Day 0 ‹ Moon Sign Sagittarius

am ....

pm ....

A definite atmosphere of involvement from others now makes it easier for you to do what appeals to you specifically. Contradictions do occur, especially in the way that you are viewing all the options for Christmas. It might be best not to try and hold too much in your slightly tired mind at once, at least today.

22 FRIDAY
Moon Age Day 1 ‹ Moon Sign Sagittarius

am ....

pm ....

You have such an abundance of energy today that there is no wonder the people you live and work with find you to be a blur of activity. Significant good luck attends most of your efforts in the month to come, as the sun takes an important trip into your solar fifth house. Secrets are safe with you, but do you want to listen?

23 SATURDAY
Moon Age Day 2 ‹ Moon Sign Capricorn

am ....

pm ....

Sometimes you work at your best when you are under a certain amount of tension, though not if you allow it to become so much a part of your life that you fail to see the wood for the trees. An atmospheric period is coming and it would be a pity if you failed to pick up on it simply because you are dealing with practicalities.

24 SUNDAY
Moon Age Day 3 ‹ Moon Sign Capricorn

am ....

pm ....

You are still in the work mode, even though this is the time to slow down. At every stage you should be willing to sit back and watch, despite the fact that in-between times you can get plenty done. A more moderate approach to the behaviour of others is something that now begins to figure in your life generally.

← *NEGATIVE TREND*						*POSITIVE TREND* →				
-5	-4	-3	-2	-1		+1	+2	+3	+4	+5
					LOVE					
					MONEY					
					LUCK					
					VITALITY					

25 MONDAY
Moon Age Day 4 ‹ Moon Sign Aquarius

am ....

pm ....

Some dramatic moments during Christmas Day do little to divert you from what turns out to be a pleasurable and rewarding day. Not everything is based around enjoyment however and there is much to be gained in the longer term from keeping your ears open to what relatives especially are trying to say to you at some stage.

26 TUESDAY
Moon Age Day 5 ‹ Moon Sign Aquarius

am ....

pm ....

With the actual day out of the way you may find it easier to settle down than was the case yesterday. If because of this all you want to do is to flop, then allow yourself the right to do so. If there are any routines to be dealt with, it would be sensible to leave them for other family members to get on with.

27 WEDNESDAY
Moon Age Day 6 ‹ Moon Sign Pisces

am ....

pm ....

The moon moves into a less favourable position. As long as there is nothing practical for you to be doing, then you can continue the possibility of a well earned rest, and without feeling guilty about the situation either. It's fair to say that for today a low profile could look more rewarding than a hectic social life.

28 THURSDAY
Moon Age Day 7 ‹ Moon Sign Pisces

am ....

pm ....

Getting together in a close one-to-one situation is apt to appeal to most Virgo subjects just at present. Romance is on your mind, and the one who cares about you the most goes along with the way that you are thinking. Make this a special time and act with foresight when thinking about the needs of family members.

29 FRIDAY
Moon Age Day 8 ‹ Moon Sign Aries

am ....

pm ....

The most routine of tasks now become a labour of love. If you are working today, put your best foot forward and make certain that all your actions are thought out well in advance of yourself. Once you have done so, there is no reason to think that anything of real importance is likely to stand in your way.

30 SATURDAY
Moon Age Day 9 ‹ Moon Sign Aries

am ....

pm ....

Unexpected social invitations are on the way, and the effect they have on your life long-term should not be underestimated now. Intellectual and mental interests take centre-stage in your life, as you look forward with a level of determination that is amazing, even for you. Accept help where it is on offer.

31 SUNDAY
Moon Age Day 10 ‹ Moon Sign Taurus

am ....

pm ....

The last day of the year shows you leaving 1995 determined to succeed even more in the time that lies ahead. New and interesting diversions come your way, thanks in part to the intervention of newcomers in your life. Parties are apt to go with a swing, and you will be there to the end of them.

← *NEGATIVE TREND*　　　　　　　　*POSITIVE TREND* →

-5	-4	-3	-2	-1		+1	+2	+3	+4	+5
					LOVE					
					MONEY					
					LUCK					
					VITALITY					

1996

YOUR MONTH AT A GLANCE

The twelve numbered boxes represent the important areas in your life.
The key to the numbers you will find beneath the panel. A Sun above
the number indicates that opportunities are around. A Cloud below
the number, that you should be a bit defensive. Nothing above or
below and life will be pretty ordinary.

	☀						☀		☀		
1	2	3	4	5	6	7	8	9	10	11	12
						☁				☁	

KEY

1 Strength of Personality
2 Personal Finance
3 Useful Information Gathering
4 Domestic Affairs
5 Pleasure & Romance
6 Effective Work & Health
7 One to One Relationships
8 Questioning, Thinking & Deciding
9 External Influences / Education
10 Career Aspirations
11 Teamwork Activities
12 Unconscious Impulses

JANUARY HIGHS AND LOWS

Here, I show how the rhythm of the Moon will affect you this month.
Like the tide, your energies and abilities will rise and fall with its pattern. When it is above the date line, go-for-it. When it is below the
line you should be resting.

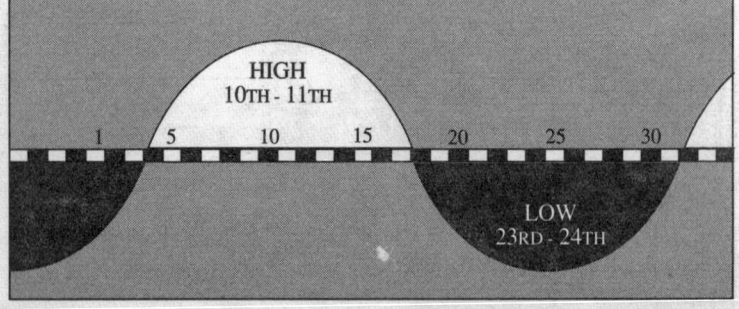

1 MONDAY   *Moon Age Day 11 • Moon Sign Taurus*

am ....

pm ....

At the start of the year some of your most rewarding moments come when you are away from the confines of your own home. It could be that you are tired of celebrations and want to talk to someone else about almost anything but having a good time. You are very committed to family members however, and help them all you can.

2 TUESDAY   *Moon Age Day 12 • Moon Sign Taurus*

am ....

pm ....

Most Virgoans should be in great demand today, both in a general and a professional sense. Remember though that you do need to make personal progress too and cannot allow yourself to be at the beck and call of everyone indefinitely. It is possible that someone will have to be disappointed.

3 WEDNESDAY   *Moon Age Day 13 • Moon Sign Gemini*

am ....

pm ....

Giant Jupiter now moves along in your solar chart, and into your fifth house. For the next twelve months or so it will occupy this position and brings with it a period when you can get much more out of loving relationships. You should be more settled but will want to start out this period in a very affectionate way.

4 THURSDAY   *Moon Age Day 14 • Moon Sign Gemini*

am ....

pm ....

Progress is possible in both a professional and a personal way today. In career matters there are new options to look at, even if these might mean a great change coming into your life. It isn't important to actually change things today, though this is an ideal opportunity to start looking at life through new eyes.

5 FRIDAY
Moon Age Day 1 5 ‹ Moon Sign Cancer

am ....

pm ....

Whilst the material and practical side of life should be running rather smoothly, the same may not turn out to be the case regarding your personal life, which could throw up a problem or two. Trying to work out how other people will react might be the most difficult thing, though Jupiter helps redress the balance.

6 SATURDAY
Moon Age Day 16 ‹ Moon Sign Cancer

am ....

pm ....

You may be reliant on the attitudes of colleagues, which is fine as long as you do not follow their plans and ideas exclusively. The giving that you are capable of now in terms of personal relationships and even friendships is offered with no strings attached, and with all your usual sensitivity.

7 SUNDAY
Moon Age Day 1 7 ‹ Moon Sign Cancer

am ....

pm ....

Personal freedom is now the name of the game, especially when it comes to being able to speak your mind in an unfettered way. Few people would try to deny you this right, and the appearance of Sunday also offers you the chance of significant rest, something which has been less likely for the last week or so.

← NEGATIVE TREND							POSITIVE TREND →			
-5	-4	-3	-2	-1		+1	+2	+3	+4	+5
					LOVE					
					MONEY					
					LUCK					
					VITALITY					

8 MONDAY
Moon Age Day 18 ‹ Moon Sign Leo

am ....

pm ....

Judgement can be somewhat clouded today, a fact that is not helped
by present movements in your solar chart. It would be a good idea
to listen to what other people have to say and then to act only after
careful consideration. Meanwhile, your domestic routines should be
comfortable and rewarding.

9 TUESDAY
Moon Age Day 19 ‹ Moon Sign Leo

am ....

pm ....

A stop and start period, though ahead of much more progressive
trends. At least if you slow things down today, you will have the
chance to think and to plan some of the actions that become more
possible in a short while. There is no shortage of useful advice
coming from the direction of loved ones and friends alike.

10 WEDNESDAY
Moon Age Day 20 ‹ Moon Sign Virgo

am ....

pm ....

The Moon is now back in your own sign of Virgo, which considering
the fact that other trends favour you too, should make for a fairly
positive combination. Luck would appear to be on your side, though
it would not be a good idea to be pushing things just for the moment.
Personally speaking, the day should be happy.

11 THURSDAY
Moon Age Day 21 ‹ Moon Sign Virgo

am ....

pm ....

Taking the initiative that exists in your mind, and the real potential
for progress, make today, and several more to come, into exactly
what you want them to be. Not a time to wait around though.
Progress depends on being in the right place at the right time, something that is quite instinctive now.

12 FRIDAY
Moon Age Day 22 ‹ Moon Sign Virgo

am ....

pm ....

The demands made upon you by others, and especially those people who are closest to you, can appear to be rather excessive now. Even so, there is an opportunity to establish a degree of intimacy with someone dear to you, much greater than would appear to have been the case for quite some time.

13 SATURDAY
Moon Age Day 23 ‹ Moon Sign Libra

am ....

pm ....

Saturday comes along, and you find yourself being pulled in two directions at the same time. One the one hand, your Virgoan qualities of tidiness and enterprise are present, whilst on the other, you have the desire to be idle across the weekend. What is most needed it seems is some sort of sensible compromise.

14 SUNDAY
Moon Age Day 24 ‹ Moon Sign Libra

am ....

pm ....

Following yesterday, take life at a steady pace, and enjoy the possibilities that are thrown up by a Sunday that means doing things in your own way. It is all too easy to run out of steam if you are expecting more of yourself than your regenerating nature is able to offer. Leave plenty of time for leisure and pleasure activities.

← *NEGATIVE TREND*   *POSITIVE TREND* →

-5	-4	-3	-2	-1			+1	+2	+3	+4	+5
					LOVE						
					MONEY						
					LUCK						
					VITALITY						

15 MONDAY   *Moon Age Day 25 ‹ Moon Sign Scorpio*

am ....

pm ....

Sweet Venus now jogs along into your solar seventh house, bringing a significant boost to personal relationships and introducing a period when you seem to be much more in charge of love affairs than has been the case in the recent past. Small efforts now have great implications further down the line.

16 TUESDAY   *Moon Age Day 26 ‹ Moon Sign Scorpio*

am ....

pm ....

Social get-togethers and group encounters of any sort prove to be especially favourable at present. It would seem that there are many people who are on the same wavelength as you are today, which should allow you to convince them of certain plans that you have been holding at the back of your mind.

17 WEDNESDAY   *Moon Age Day 27 ‹ Moon Sign Sagittarius*

am ....

pm ....

An emotional issue can prove to be a little disappointing now, but probably not for long. Enterprise and enthusiasm for professional issues are better accented, and it is in this direction that you should probably be looking. Confidence to do the right thing could be greater than it at first seems to be.

18 THURSDAY   *Moon Age Day 28 ‹ Moon Sign Sagittarius*

am ....

pm ....

This could be the best day of the week for getting together with friends. Many of the possibilities are happening in a surprising way, so it is important to watch carefully and to react accordingly. Co-operative ventures are well starred and offer the chance of improving your lot in a financial sense.

19 FRIDAY

Moon Age Day 29 ‹ Moon Sign Capricorn

am ....

pm ....

The Sun, such an important component in anyone's chart, now moves slowly into your fifth house. Now we find a period of greater personal prominence and a time when others are much more likely to listen carefully to all you have to say. Reaching sensible conclusions about anything is not difficult in the month ahead.

20 SATURDAY

Moon Age Day 0 ‹ Moon Sign Capricorn

am ....

pm ....

A multitude of small aspects now work heavily in your favour and it is important to realise how easy it would be to make faulty judgements. Current plans need to be looked at carefully, though without withdrawing your recent efforts to establish a more adventurous routine and better prospects.

21 SUNDAY

Moon Age Day 1 ‹ Moon Sign Aquarius

am ....

pm ....

Because you can be a sensitive type, you should be able to notice any emotional undercurrents that are apparent within the family. Dealing with such matters now, while you are in the mood, could be very important. In many more practical respects it would be good to strike whilst the iron is hot!

← NEGATIVE TREND							POSITIVE TREND →			
-5	-4	-3	-2	-1			+1	+2	+3	+4	+5
					LOVE						
					MONEY						
					LUCK						
					VITALITY						

22 MONDAY   *Moon Age Day 2 ‹ Moon Sign Aquarius*

am ....

pm ....

Today's combination of influences help to bring out the best in you, and put to sleep for a while the more pedantic qualities of your sign. You tend to be relaxed and easy-going, facts that increase your popularity no end at present. When you are out and about, which is often, you can create a very good impression.

23 TUESDAY   *Moon Age Day 3 ‹ Moon Sign Pisces*

am ....

pm ....

The remarks that others make could well have more of an impact on you than should reasonably be expected to be the case at present. It appears that certain people are letting you down, though you may come to realise that much of the problem lies in the way that you look at things. Take time out to watch.

24 WEDNESDAY   *Moon Age Day 4 ‹ Moon Sign Pisces*

am ....

pm ....

The Moon is not in a very good position for those of you who may want to make very real forward progress just at present. Occupying your opposite sign, the Moon prompts you to take on a quieter phase, and one that responds much better to thinking about situations, rather than participating too much.

25 THURSDAY   *Moon Age Day 5 ‹ Moon Sign Aries*

am ....

pm ....

Travel should be at the forefront of your mind. Even if it is not possible or desirable to be getting away just at present, you could be doing some planning for a later date. You are not too far away from a definite mental peak, when it should be easier in a general sense to look ahead.

26 FRIDAY

Moon Age Day 6 ‹ Moon Sign Aries

am ....

pm ....

You will have to get priorities right now, from the very start of the day. Anyone who is in a position to be of help to you will almost certainly come good at this time, and you find that there is all the help you could need to forge new professional and personal ties. Look out for more dubious types however.

27 SATURDAY

Moon Age Day 7 ‹ Moon Sign Taurus

am ....

pm ....

Professional matters are apt to put additional strain on you, perhaps more in your mind than in reality on this winter Saturday. It would be a good idea to forget all about work for a day or two if you can, opting instead for a family time, with diversions galore, once you take the trouble to look for them.

28 SUNDAY

Moon Age Day 8 ‹ Moon Sign Taurus

am ....

pm ....

It is still the weekend, and you need to make certain that you are not pushing yourself along at a greater rate than you instinctively know to be either sensible or possible. With an extra effort, apply the brakes on life and, for the rest of today at least, make it do what you want it to. Tomorrow comes soon enough.

← NEGATIVE TREND						POSITIVE TREND →				
-5	-4	-3	-2	-1		+1	+2	+3	+4	+5
					LOVE					
					MONEY					
					LUCK					
					VITALITY					

29 MONDAY   *Moon Age Day 9 ‹ Moon Sign Taurus*

am ....

pm ....

Beware of hasty financial decisions and take your time over making
any definite changes in your life for the moment. People are relying
quite heavily on your experience and knowledge of life and you
should find that even normally awkward types are willing to follow
the examples that you are able to set.

30 TUESDAY   *Moon Age Day 10 ‹ Moon Sign Gemini*

am ....

pm ....

Some Virgoans find themselves at the start of a positive new phase
in terms of romantic attachments and favourable relationships
generally. You are moderate in your opinions, but well able to
predict how others will behave under almost any given circumstance. Don't give in to idle fancies however.

31 WEDNESDAY   *Moon Age Day 11 ‹ Moon Sign Gemini*

am ....

pm ....

The need for variety and interest in your day-to-day life is extremely
well emphasized at present. Making up your mind as you go along,
you can really respond to off-the-cuff suggestions and to the interesting schemes of those people who normally tend to rely on you. Avoid
the urge to rush anything at all.

1 THURSDAY   *Moon Age Day 12 ‹ Moon Sign Cancer*

am ....

pm ....

Social group involvements are definitely to the fore right now. You
still have plenty of energy at your disposal and are keen to project
some of it out into the world as a whole, where you find plenty of
people happy to go along with your ideas. A number of people take
you up now on schemes from some time past.

2 FRIDAY   *Moon Age Day 13 ‹ Moon Sign Cancer*

am ....

pm ....

Although career matters and general responsibilities are apt to take
a heavy toll on you at present, this is no reason to throw out the
baby with the bathwater by ignoring your social life. If anything has
to give it should be the practical aspects of the day. Take a few
hours out to simply please yourself.

3 SATURDAY   *Moon Age Day 14 ‹ Moon Sign Cancer*

am ....

pm ....

This first weekend of February offers you the chance to sit back and
watch. New and better deals are possible if you are determined to
go out shopping, but you do also need to make certain that any docu-
ment you sing is working in your favour. It is possible to be duped
at present, so some extra care counts.

4 SUNDAY   *Moon Age Day 15 ‹ Moon Sign Leo*

am ....

pm ....

It would be wise at present, especially with the trends that now
predominate in your chart, not to force issues of any kind when in
social get-togethers. Time spent with friends or family should be
kept as casual as possible and there is no real reason to be facing up
to harsh, practical realities for now.

← *NEGATIVE TREND*   *POSITIVE TREND* →

-5	-4	-3	-2	-1			+1	+2	+3	+4	+5
					LOVE						
					MONEY						
					LUCK						
					VITALITY						

1996

YOUR MONTH AT A GLANCE

The twelve numbered boxes represent the important areas in your life.
The key to the numbers you will find beneath the panel. A Sun above
the number indicates that opportunities are around. A Cloud below
the number, that you should be a bit defensive. Nothing above or
below and life will be pretty ordinary.

					☀					☀	☀
1	2	3	4	5	6	7	8	9	10	11	12
							☁		☁		

```
                         KEY
1 Strength of Personality      7 One to One Relationships
2 Personal Finance             8 Questioning, Thinking & Deciding
3 Useful Information Gathering  9 External Influences / Education
4 Domestic Affairs             10 Career Aspirations
5 Pleasure & Romance           11 Teamwork Activities
6 Effective Work & Health      12 Unconscious Impulses
```

FEBRUARY HIGHS AND LOWS

Here, I show how the rhythm of the Moon will affect you this month.
Like the tide, your energies and abilities will rise and fall with its pattern. When it is above the date line, go-for-it. When it is below the
line you should be resting.

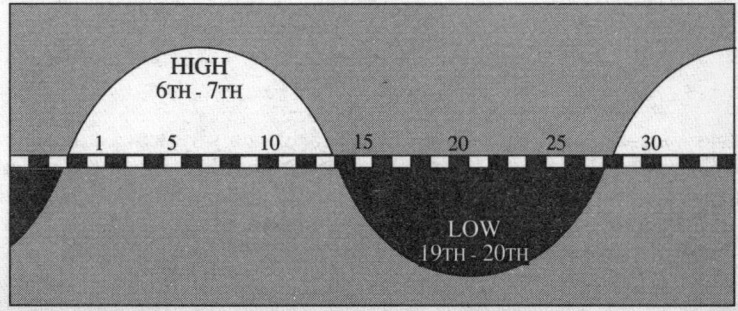

5 MONDAY
Moon Age Day 16 • Moon Sign Leo

am ....

pm ....

Largely an introvertive sort of day, when the quieter qualities of your chart really are in evidence. You don't have too much enthusiasm for new projects and would be better off simply resting and waiting until trends improve. There is always someone around who is willing to help you out at the moment.

6 TUESDAY
Moon Age Day 17 • Moon Sign Virgo

am ....

pm ....

Be on the lookout for new acquaintances and friends who can brighten up your day no end. Time away from emotional ties that have proved to be rather demanding of late would not be a bad thing. Whatever you decide to do, you should not feel guilty for taking a course of action that you know is right.

7 WEDNESDAY
Moon Age Day 18 • Moon Sign Virgo

am ....

pm ....

The lunar high arrives again, and happy you will be to have it so. Probably suddenly, your level of energy is on the increase, and this is a time to put into action one or two of the plans that have been held in abeyance for a while. Neither do you have to look all that far in order to find suitable assistance.

8 THURSDAY
Moon Age Day 19 • Moon Sign Virgo

am ....

pm ....

Most Virgoans will find themselves reaching a physical peak today, so there should be plenty of entertaining possibilities to take your fancy. Most of the tasks that you decide to undertake are dealt with quickly and efficiently, leaving you with plenty of time to do whatever takes your fancy later in the day.

9 FRIDAY

Moon Age Day 20 ‹ Moon Sign Libra

am ....

pm ....

The best in you is now on show. Rules and regulations do get on your nerves, but you manage to find sensible ways to sidestep them and to do what you feel is right in an hour by hour sense. It might be sensible to reserve just a little of your drive and determination until the weekend however. Friends are subtle now.

10 SATURDAY

Moon Age Day 21 ‹ Moon Sign Libra

am ....

pm ....

You are at your most comfortable now in domestic situations, so you could opt for a stay-at-home sort of weekend. Emotionally you will not want to do anything that means rocking the boat and could easily be looking for an easier life. There might be some benefit from a shopping expedition and the chance to treat yourself a little.

11 SUNDAY

Moon Age Day 22 ‹ Moon Sign Scorpio

am ....

pm ....

Friends could have some interesting news that may perk up your weekend significantly. The only problem might be that if you don't ask, you are never going to discover what is really going on. This is one of the reasons why you will want to be at the forefront of possibilities today and tomorrow.

← *NEGATIVE TREND*   *POSITIVE TREND* →

-5	-4	-3	-2	-1		+1	+2	+3	+4	+5
					LOVE					
					MONEY					
					LUCK					
					VITALITY					

12 MONDAY

Moon Age Day 23 ‹ Moon Sign Scorpio

am ....

pm ....

Don't try to mix business and pleasure. This is not to say that there cannot be some of each today, but merely that you need to keep them separate for the moment. By the evening, you should be quite happy to sit and put your feet up for a while. Friends and acquaintances alike find you particularly attractive at present.

13 TUESDAY

Moon Age Day 24 ‹ Moon Sign Sagittarius

am ....

pm ....

It would be a good idea, for today at least, to allow your partner to take most of the major decisions associated with house and home. Look towards a quieter period, in which case you can enjoy a relaxing time in the company of those you care about the most, without feeling that you have to make a special effort.

14 WEDNESDAY

Moon Age Day 25 ‹ Moon Sign Sagittarius

am ....

pm ....

High spirits are clearly in evidence now, mainly thanks to the position of little Mercury in your solar fifth house. Your romantic and material life benefits from the present trends and you can push your mind forward towards a time when it is possible to take your most cherished plans and make them come alive.

15 THURSDAY

Moon Age Day 26 ‹ Moon Sign Capricorn

am ....

pm ....

All discussions should be turned to your advantage today, especially those that deal with your future in a professional sense. Get busy with practical matters too, since the level of your physical energy is apt to be quite high. The one thing that you cannot afford to do is to waste time in pointless speculation.

16 FRIDAY   *Moon Age Day 27 ‹ Moon Sign Capricorn*

am ....

pm ....

Your ability to make situations go in the directions that you would
wish is now especially emphasised. The need for comfort and
security at home could distract you from taking the direction that is
most profitable, but friends and associates seem determined that you
should do your best, partly for them.

17 SATURDAY   *Moon Age Day 28 ‹ Moon Sign Aquarius*

am ....

pm ....

Personal and professional involvements may be less satisfying than
you had desired, and you do need to feel very involved emotionally
with whatever is going on around you. There is more positivity in
your attitude and you should be able to find absorbing and
interesting things to do. Tedious jobs should be performed early.

18 SUNDAY   *Moon Age Day 29 ‹ Moon Sign Aquarius*

am ....

pm ....

A general improvement to relationships should continue to be
noticed. Planets are in an ideal position to help you out now, and is
especially good in the area of communication. This would be as
useful a time as any to take the initiative in personal attachments,
with sound advice at your finger-tips.

← NEGATIVE TREND   *POSITIVE TREND →*

-5	-4	-3	-2	-1		+1	+2	+3	+4	+5
					LOVE					
					MONEY					
					LUCK					
					VITALITY					

19 MONDAY

Moon Age Day 0 ‹ Moon Sign Aquarius

am ....

pm ....

Information regarding professional involvements start the week favourably and future plans put you in the picture allowing you to lay down new ground rules for your own life. Beware, loved ones could be feeling neglected and in need of special attention that you are able to give. Former associates begin to become close friends.

20 TUESDAY

Moon Age Day 1 ‹ Moon Sign Pisces

am ....

pm ....

Expect some particularly happy news from a partner or from foreign parts. Social discussions are especially agreeable and rewarding whilst your outlook on life can be influenced especially in a financial sense by your partner or someone who clearly has your best interests at heart. Deep concentration can be difficult.

21 WEDNESDAY

Moon Age Day 2 ‹ Moon Sign Pisces

am ....

pm ....

Certainly a good day for getting down to basics and for settling any misunderstandings that exist in your vicinity. Because you are communicating clearly and logically, those closest to you are willing to listen to what you have to say. You really do exhibit a human touch and this reflects favourably in most endeavours.

22 THURSDAY

Moon Age Day 3 ‹ Moon Sign Aries

am ....

pm ....

Conflicting interests attend your life now with career and family responsibilities at odds with each other. From the very start of the day it is important to get your priorities right and attend to the issues that mean the most to you at any particular point in time. A close family member may require emotional support.

23 FRIDAY

Moon Age Day 4 ‹ Moon Sign Aries

am ....

pm ....

Some people appear to do their best to let you down. In reality this has more to do with the way that you are feeling inside yourself. You may not feel very much like confronting personal issues today, but in fact this would be a good time to get them out in the open and sorted out.

24 SATURDAY

Moon Age Day 5 ‹ Moon Sign Taurus

am ....

pm ....

It seems as if your personal judgement is called into question by people in your immediate vicinity. The last thing you should do is take a 'know-it-all' approach. Your imagination is stimulated and you grow stronger in your ability to visualise a brighter and better future for yourself and for those around you.

25 SUNDAY

Moon Age Day 6 ‹ Moon Sign Taurus

am ....

pm ....

Arguments are possible in a social sense, due to a tendency to take remarks personally. However, later in the day the shoe may be on the other foot since it is you that is giving offence. Whilst feelings of others need to be taken into consideration your own attitude towards life is rather strange at present and should not be taken seriously.

← *NEGATIVE TREND*   *POSITIVE TREND* →

-5	-4	-3	-2	-1			+1	+2	+3	+4	+5
					LOVE						
					MONEY						
					LUCK						
					VITALITY						

26 MONDAY

Moon Age Day 7 ‹ Moon Sign Gemini

am ....

pm ....

Although many of you will be back in harness today, in reality this would be a great time to be seeking out some personal choice in your life. All prospects for travel are very good and those Virgoans who have chosen to take a break this week may turn out to be the luckiest of all. Friends behave very sensibly.

27 TUESDAY

Moon Age Day 8 ‹ Moon Sign Gemini

am ....

pm ....

It could be that you prefer a lower profile today than has been the case recently, concentrating on private matters and mulling over situations from the past. However, despite your need for privacy and independence, you should be careful not to shut others out totally.

28 WEDNESDAY

Moon Age Day 9 ‹ Moon Sign Gemini

am ....

pm ....

Those in authority place you in a rather taxing role today, but this does at least offer you the opportunity to show how efficient you can be. Efforts today can lead towards a better destination that you had expected and so you will be doing all you can to prove your worth in every respect.

29 THURSDAY

Moon Age Day 10 ‹ Moon Sign Cancer

am ....

pm ....

You seem to be enjoying a particularly high profile in the outside world. The only danger here is that you are inclined to take on too much in the way of commitments. Confrontations, particularly with powerful types should be avoided and conciliation is always the best course of action for you at present. Contrary opinions are possible.

1 FRIDAY

Moon Age Day 11 ‹ Moon Sign Cancer

am ....

pm ....

Colleagues and associates can be in a difficult or unapproachable
mood, but this should not prevent progress as far as you are
concerned personally. It will be not only difficult, but probably
impossible to check the behaviour of others and the best course of
action is simply to let them be. Not a time for taking many risks.

2 SATURDAY

Moon Age Day 12 ‹ Moon Sign Leo

am ....

pm ....

Group efforts and co-operation of all sorts pay dividends. Help
comes in from the outside world and provides excellent progress
generally. Social involvements provide a happy atmosphere where
you can forget about the cares of the world and concentrate more on
your own personal desires.

3 SUNDAY

Moon Age Day 13 ‹ Moon Sign Leo

am ....

pm ....

Today could be a little dramatic in a personal sense, especially if you
decide that a good heart-to-heart is required. Try to get others to
confide in you, as this will be the only way that you can be of real
help to anyone. When it comes to planning of a more professional
nature, the day can be very useful.

← *NEGATIVE TREND*   FUN   *POSITIVE TREND* →

-5	-4	-3	-2	-1			+1	+2	+3	+4	+5
					LOVE						
					MONEY						
					LUCK						
					VITALITY						

1996

YOUR MONTH AT A GLANCE

The twelve numbered boxes represent the important areas in your life.
The key to the numbers you will find beneath the panel. A Sun above
the number indicates that opportunities are around. A Cloud below
the number, that you should be a bit defensive. Nothing above or
below and life will be pretty ordinary.

1	2	3	4	5	6	7	8	9	10	11	12

Suns above: 2, 4, 5. Clouds below: 7, 10.

KEY

1 Strength of Personality	7 One to One Relationships
2 Personal Finance	8 Questioning, Thinking & Deciding
3 Useful Information Gathering	9 External Influences / Education
4 Domestic Affairs	10 Career Aspirations
5 Pleasure & Romance	11 Teamwork Activities
6 Effective Work & Health	12 Unconscious Impulses

MARCH HIGHS AND LOWS

Here, I show how the rhythm of the Moon will affect you this month.
Like the tide, your energies and abilities will rise and fall with its pattern. When it is above the date line, go-for-it. When it is below the
line you should be resting.

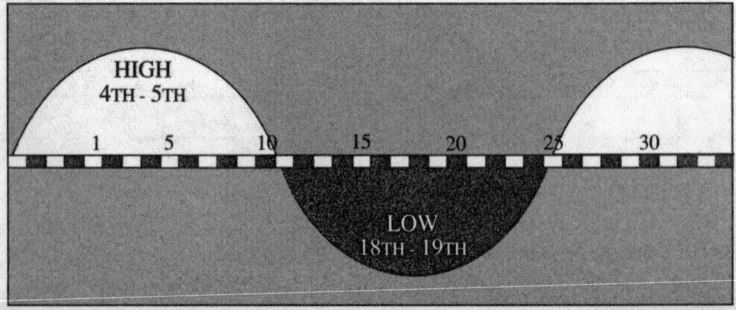

HIGH
4TH - 5TH

LOW
18TH - 19TH

4 MONDAY
Moon Age Day 14 • Moon Sign Leo

am ....

pm ....

The arrival of the lunar high represents the beginning of a new cycle when fresh starts become ever more likely. This is especially true with regard to your personal life and since luck is also on your side, you can even afford to take the odd chance. However, many of the benefits of the period may not prove to be particularly obvious today.

5 TUESDAY
Moon Age Day 15 • Moon Sign Virgo

am ....

pm ....

Not only can you be inspired by almost anything that is going on around you, but you have a profound effect on the opinions and attitudes of others. Taking risks could prove to be fortunate, though keep these to a minimum for the moment. All opportunities that arise in a professional sense should be turned to your advantage.

6 WEDNESDAY
Moon Age Day 16 • Moon Sign Virgo

am ....

pm ....

There is a degree of uncertainty regarding business or professional aspects of your life. Take note - it would be unwise to make any important moves unless you are absolutely certain of your direction in life. Keeping to a tried and tested path is important and more than ever it is better to be safe than sorry today.

7 THURSDAY
Moon Age Day 17 • Moon Sign Libra

am ....

pm ....

Information that you may have been expecting from the direction of loved ones is a little slow in arriving, if it turns up at all. Confidence to do the right thing in any given situation is not forthcoming either and in many situations you will have no choice but to fall back on your intuition.

8 FRIDAY
Moon Age Day 18‹ Moon Sign Libra

am ....

pm ....

A combination of planetary interactions do much to stimulate the pleasure-seeking qualities of your nature, though could also make you rather too inclined to seek the sensational in life. Continuity is important in a working sense, though don't ignore the fact that the weekend is only a day away.

9 SATURDAY
Moon Age Day 19 ‹ Moon Sign Scorpio

am ....

pm ....

Any conflict today arises as a result of your desire to be of use to family and friends and your need to be busy in a practical sense too. It should be possible to split the day, allowing you to do all that is requires. What you won't manage is to divide yourself in half in an emotional sense.

10 SUNDAY
Moon Age Day 20 ‹ Moon Sign Scorpio

am ....

pm ....

A Sunday that finds you fairly contented with your lot. Working Virgoans have some benefits in store, though even if you have some time to spare you will not be short of something constructive to do. A bold attitude can work wonders when you are confronted by people with a very definite point of view.

← *NEGATIVE TREND*							*POSITIVE TREND* →			
-5	-4	-3	-2	-1		+1	+2	+3	+4	+5
					LOVE					
					MONEY					
					LUCK					
					VITALITY					

11 MONDAY

Moon Age Day 21 ‹ Moon Sign Scorpio

am ....

pm ....

Benefits accrue and life should be fairly smooth for you today, even if there are one or two people about who appear to be determined to throw a spanner in the works. Conversation is both interesting and informative and there are aspects to new relationships that could easily surprise you at some stage.

12 TUESDAY

Moon Age Day 22 ‹ Moon Sign Sagittarius

am ....

pm ....

It's back to basics today if you want to make the sort of progress that has been required for some time. Catch up with any unfinished business as soon as you can and don't allow yourself to be diverted from those jobs that you know to be of real importance. You really do have your sensible head on now.

13 WEDNESDAY

Moon Age Day 23 ‹ Moon Sign Sagittarius

am ....

pm ....

An over-confident attitude, no doubt brought about by some favourable trends that have been around for a while, now makes itself felt. The trouble here is that you may find yourself launching all sorts of new ventures that you are not really ready to deal with just yet. Slow and steady is the way forward now.

14 THURSDAY

Moon Age Day 24 ‹ Moon Sign Capricorn

am ....

pm ....

Although you are probably in a more quiet mood that would generally be the case for your sign at present, you can already feel subtle undertones that indicate a change back to a more gregarious state of affairs. Your intuitive powers tend to be quite strong at present, so be willing to back your hunches.

15 FRIDAY

Moon Age Day 25 ‹ Moon Sign Capricorn

am ....

pm ....

All career and professional matters work best today if everyone decides from the outset to pull together. It may be up to you to make certain that this happens, and to encourage everyone concerned to keep the ultimate objectives in mind. This should give good impetus to the end of the working week.

16 SATURDAY

Moon Age Day 26 ‹ Moon Sign Aquarius

am ....

pm ....

Now that the weekend is here you could have decided that this is the time for making changes in and around your home. Your competence and practical energies are high, reinforcing such thoughts and making you more than usually aware of the needs and wants of your family.

17 SUNDAY

Moon Age Day 27 ‹ Moon Sign Aquarius

am ....

pm ....

There is no difficulty in attracting the good things of life today, or indeed for a day or two to come. Still there is a certain dissatisfaction about the way that you see things and possibly a slight problem if you indulge yourself too much in any way. Basically life should be fairly happy however.

← NEGATIVE TREND							POSITIVE TREND →			
-5	-4	-3	-2	-1		+1	+2	+3	+4	+5
					LOVE					
					MONEY					
					LUCK					
					VITALITY					

18 MONDAY   *Moon Age Day 28 ‹ Moon Sign Pisces*

am ....

pm ....

The lunar low does bring a dip in practical affairs, though this time
round it should do little to curb your enthusiasm for social
encounters of any sort. Although there are certain niggles at the
back of your mind you should be fairly happy, and especially so in a
strictly personal sense later in the day.

19 TUESDAY   *Moon Age Day 0 ‹ Moon Sign Pisces*

am ....

pm ....

Life is still apt to be quiet, and that means time to think things
through and to come to terms with present changes. Small mishaps
in routine matters are of no real importance, though they may cause
you to think slightly differently about certain aspects of your life.
Personal confidence is restored in no time.

20 WEDNESDAY   *Moon Age Day 1 ‹ Moon Sign Aries*

am ....

pm ....

Although you may consider that your opinions are valid, other
people could have rather different ideas at present. You do show a
slight tendency towards pessimism, a fact that is not very useful
when it comes to turning situations around, or making your friends
aware of your real point-of-view.

21 THURSDAY   *Moon Age Day 2 ‹ Moon Sign Aries*

am ....

pm ....

It is time for some quick thinking and decisive actions in relation to
your personal life. Once you have had time to think things over, act
instantly since hesitation should be avoided in all spheres of your life
at present. Don't allow moods or an over-emotional phase to cloud
your judgement and try to stay calm, even if provoked.

22 FRIDAY

Moon Age Day 3 ‹ Moon Sign Taurus

am ....

pm ....

Because you are keeping a fairly low profile, you should also have the time to attend to any unfinished tasks or duties. Relationships prove to be favourable as you are presently surrounded by warm-hearted people. A new love might come as a surprise to Virgoans who are open to romantic suggestions.

23 SATURDAY

Moon Age Day 4 ‹ Moon Sign Taurus

am ....

pm ....

Just when things seem to be running quite smoothly, issues from the past surface again and threaten to hold you back. A more taxing role personally is indicated and this is not a time to give in to negative thinking. Forcing yourself forward is not too easy, and may even turn out to be something of a waste of time in the end.

24 SUNDAY

Moon Age Day 5 ‹ Moon Sign Taurus

am ....

pm ....

It might be difficult to find yourself in the company of particularly entertaining types this Sunday, though even routine contacts can prove profitable at the moment. With trends generally working for you, you should be feeling good about life in general, and could also be on the receiving end of minor financial gains.

← *NEGATIVE TREND*　　　　　　*POSITIVE TREND* →

-5	-4	-3	-2	-1		+1	+2	+3	+4	+5
					LOVE					
					MONEY					
					LUCK					
					VITALITY					

25 MONDAY   *Moon Age Day 6 ‹ Moon Sign Gemini*

am ....

pm ....

On what is not a specifically adventurous day, it is important to keep to tried and trusted paths, consolidating gains that have already been made rather than considering fresh ideas. There are many occasions when you will have to rely on your own wit and resources to make progress possible.

26 TUESDAY   *Moon Age Day 7 ‹ Moon Sign Gemini*

am ....

pm ....

The pendulum swings again and some especially noteworthy happenings bring a higher profile and an increase in the pace of everyday life. Much can be achieved at this time and positive thinking assists you to retain an air of confidence concerning your own plans and ideas.

27 WEDNESDAY   *Moon Age Day 8 ‹ Moon Sign Cancer*

am ....

pm ....

There is absolutely no lack of optimism today and the possibility of any change of scene is very welcome. Broaden your horizons through becoming involved in social gatherings and don't be generally reluctant to say what you think, even if to do so is going against the grain from someone else's point of view.

28 THURSDAY   *Moon Age Day 9 ‹ Moon Sign Cancer*

am ....

pm ....

Maintaining a positive self-image, it is fairly easy for you to attract others to you through the sheer force of your present personality. Some practical matters and ambitions show signs of significant success and long term plans can be brought to completion. Health and vitality look better than for some days.

29 FRIDAY

Moon Age Day 10 ‹ Moon Sign Cancer

am ....

pm ....

At the end of this working week, it is all too easy to be misunderstood today, particularly in terms of your work and practical matters at home. Part of the problem may lay in the fact that other people see you as a competitor even though this is not what you intend to be. A few gentle words of reassurance help.

30 SATURDAY

Moon Age Day 11 ‹ Moon Sign Leo

am ....

pm ....

The pleasure seeking Virgoan now puts in a definite appearance. You do have to guard against the temptation to go over the top financially, particularly with regard to leisure of luxury items. Excitement is possible romantically and you are definitely flavour of the month in some important person's world.

31 SUNDAY

Moon Age Day 12 ‹ Moon Sign Leo

am ....

pm ....

There may be no real explanation for the way you feel today, merely lacking in energy and unable to make the progress that you are looking for. You should be prepared to take a back-seat and let others do the running. This is the time to recharge your batteries, even though you may never know why.

	NEGATIVE TREND						POSITIVE TREND			
-5	-4	-3	-2	-1		+1	+2	+3	+4	+5
					LOVE					
					MONEY					
					LUCK					
					VITALITY					

1996

YOUR MONTH AT A GLANCE

The twelve numbered boxes represent the important areas in your life.
The key to the numbers you will find beneath the panel. A Sun above
the number indicates that opportunities are around. A Cloud below
the number, that you should be a bit defensive. Nothing above or
below and life will be pretty ordinary.

	☀					☀	☀				
1	2	3	4	5	6	7	8	9	10	11	12
								☁		☁	

KEY

1 Strength of Personality
2 Personal Finance
3 Useful Information Gathering
4 Domestic Affairs
5 Pleasure & Romance
6 Effective Work & Health

7 One to One Relationships
8 Questioning, Thinking & Deciding
9 External Influences / Education
10 Career Aspirations
11 Teamwork Activities
12 Unconscious Impulses

APRIL HIGHS AND LOWS

Here, I show how the rhythm of the Moon will affect you this month.
Like the tide, your energies and abilities will rise and fall with its pattern. When it is above the date line, go-for-it. When it is below the
line you should be resting.

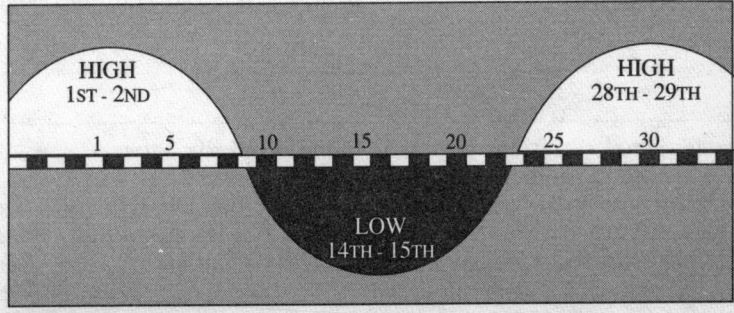

1 MONDAY

Moon Age Day 13 • Moon Sign Virgo

am ....

pm ....

An important start to the year, with the Moon still in your own sign and plenty working in your favour. Of course, whether or not you decide to make full use of the potential is up to you. Events now tend to confirm your past beliefs and make your path through life in the days ahead that much easier.

2 TUESDAY

Moon Age Day 14 • Moon Sign Virgo

am ....

pm ....

Serious decisions are needed now and you will not want to delay them any longer than is really necessary. Spread your wings a little in the times when you are not actually taking on more responsibility because you do need to establish some rest periods to compensate for busy times.

3 WEDNESDAY

Moon Age Day 15 • Moon Sign Libra

am ....

pm ....

Challenges from others, about issues that are really important, cannot be ignored or shelved. You have to face the world head on at present, and you will be determined to come out as the winner. This is one time when the stubborn qualities of Virgo turn out to be a distinct advantage, but only if they are used wisely.

4 THURSDAY

Moon Age Day 16 • Moon Sign Libra

am ....

pm ....

Professional situations appear to improve greatly between now and the weekend, and it's really down to the fact that you are still putting your ideas across in a considered and sensible way. You don't put up with too much criticism it's true, though others recognise the fact and may not take you to task at all.

5 FRIDAY
Moon Age Day 17 ‹ Moon Sign Libra

am ....

pm ....

Your love life and pleasure activities are very much the fore now and there should be plenty of excitement throughout the day if you are able to go out and look for it. It might appear that others are unwilling to do what they can on your behalf, though in the fullness of time they are more flexible.

6 SATURDAY
Moon Age Day 18 ‹ Moon Sign Scorpio

am ....

pm ....

Information could go astray today, and for reasons that are difficult, if not impossible, to understand. All in all, it isn't really worth the time to look at things too deeply and you would be far better advised just to get on, and where it is necessary to commence projects from the beginning again.

7 SUNDAY
Moon Age Day 19 ‹ Moon Sign Scorpio

am ....

pm ....

It could be rather difficult to get your own way with loved ones at present and the best course of action would be to allow them a degree of self-choice. You could find them to be more sensible now than you have reason to believe would be the case. The past makes a very bad yard-stick for judging the present today.

← NEGATIVE TREND							POSITIVE TREND →				
-5	-4	-3	-2	-1		+1	+2	+3	+4	+5
					LOVE					
					MONEY					
					LUCK					
					VITALITY					

8 MONDAY
Moon Age Day 20 ‹ Moon Sign Sagittarius

am ....

pm ....

An association between Venus and the planet Uranus happening now shows how very easy it is to get your head into gear regarding all professional matters at the start of this new working week. Today may not be particularly eventful in itself, though it is possible for you to take decisions that are far-reaching.

9 TUESDAY
Moon Age Day 21 ‹ Moon Sign Sagittarius

am ....

pm ....

You can take advantage of passing good luck and get yourself into the mood for activity of all kinds. Love relationships have rarely been better than they seem to be at present and they do respond well to the sort of effort that you are putting into life generally. Confidence strengthens and grows rapidly.

10 WEDNESDAY
Moon Age Day 22 ‹ Moon Sign Capricorn

am ....

pm ....

There should be a general lightening of the mood of those around you today, which can only contribute to your general sense of wellbeing and happiness. As always, there are those around who would wish to throw a slight spanner in the works, but they are unlikely to have too much of a bearing on your thoughts.

11 THURSDAY
Moon Age Day 23 ‹ Moon Sign Capricorn

am ....

pm ....

Perhaps the best day of the month for romantic encounters of any sort. A boost to your ego comes courtesy of the advice and help being offered by a friend and that means the start of an especially good interlude in a personal sense. It's really amazing just how much you can get from even casual conversations.

12 FRIDAY *Moon Age Day 24 ‹ Moon Sign Aquarius*

am ....

pm ....

Some discussions can fail to get you anywhere, and it might be worthwhile to stop short of putting in more effort than you really have to in this direction. Working on slowly and steadily, perhaps even on your own, is far better than pointless arguments which are going to be impossible for you to win.

13 SATURDAY *Moon Age Day 25 ‹ Moon Sign Aquarius*

am ....

pm ....

One-to-one relationships are particularly rewarding at the present time and allow you to plumb the depths of your own emotional nature. No doubt there are a number of compliments coming your way and you will want to do all that you can to show affection to the people who figure prominently in you life.

14 SUNDAY *Moon Age Day 26 ‹ Moon Sign Pisces*

am ....

pm ....

Beware of making snap financial decisions, especially in a business sense. This is probably less than likely on a Sunday, though it is true to say that your desire nature in a number of directions is strongly stimulated at present. However, be careful of demanding more than your fair share of everything and avoid possessiveness.

15 MONDAY
Moon Age Day 27 ‹ Moon Sign Pisces

am ....

pm ....

You are not working at your best today, and if you notice this fact you can also take heart from the fact that the Moon is presently in your opposite zodiac sign, a situations that only lasts for a day or two. This is a time to rest, reflect and to make plans for more personally fortunate periods than today.

16 TUESDAY
Moon Age Day 28 ‹ Moon Sign Aries

am ....

pm ....

It is possible that you could feel that you owe it to colleagues or friends to assist in their plans, or to perform some special favour on their behalf. Imagination is probably what leads the field here, though you cannot really lose out by giving someone a surprise in any case. You contribute to general happiness now.

17 WEDNESDAY
Moon Age Day 0 ‹ Moon Sign Aries

am ....

pm ....

Whatever you decide you want to do today, there is every indications that you do it with your heart, as well as your head. All the more reason to find yourself in the position of supporting loved ones and friends alike. Even people who are not particularly supportive are likely to be more cooperative now.

18 THURSDAY
Moon Age Day 1 ‹ Moon Sign Aries

am ....

pm ....

Although a good and generally productive day, present trends show that you have a tendency to over-work yourself physically. What you are doing is appreciated by others and particularly superiors, though loved ones may be less impressed and could try to force you into a more relaxing phase.

19 FRIDAY

Moon Age Day 2 ‹ Moon Sign Taurus

am ....

pm ....

Financial fluctuations are inevitable today, and you would be well advised not to speculate more than is necessary, if at all. You are just not seeing things as clearly as you might and would really kick yourself later if you made some glaring mistake now. Greater confidence is possible in romantic situations.

20 SATURDAY

Moon Age Day 3 ‹ Moon Sign Taurus

am ....

pm ....

This is a day of minor, though significant, personal success. Although it would still not be wise to speculate too much. Most of the benefits that attend you today are as a result of past efforts, although you can also use today as a significant platform from which to launch yourself into the future.

21 SUNDAY

Moon Age Day 4 ‹ Moon Sign Gemini

am ....

pm ....

A slightly less favourable trend today, with less domestic potential than usual for a weekend. Remember though, especially with this being Sunday, you are in charge of what is going on in your own life and you do not have to do things that go definitely against the grain. Plans fare much better in the light of enthusiasm.

← NEGATIVE TREND							POSITIVE TREND →			
-5	-4	-3	-2	-1			+1	+2	+3	+4	+5
					LOVE						
					MONEY						
					LUCK						
					VITALITY						

22 MONDAY
Moon Age Day 5 ‹ Moon Sign Gemini

am ....

pm ....

Your present natural restlessness is now inclined to increase, which can make for a slightly less than comfortable start to the working week. Perhaps you should think in terms of doing something different and putting the practicalities of life on the back burner for just a short while. Sidestep an argument.

23 TUESDAY
Moon Age Day 6 ‹ Moon Sign Cancer

am ....

pm ....

Look forward to some important advancements in both personal and professional endeavours. Venus is in your solar tenth house, which affords you the sort of popularity that could be of great use. You now tend to push your efforts into directions that you know are likely to pay the greatest dividends later on.

24 WEDNESDAY
Moon Age Day 7 ‹ Moon Sign Cancer

am ....

pm ....

There is little doubt that a fairly low profile works best for you and indeed you may not even have the desire to deal with others to the extent that would normally be the case. Be especially careful with anyone who appears too good to be true as there is a distinct possibility that they are somehow deceptive.

25 THURSDAY
Moon Age Day 8 ‹ Moon Sign Cancer

am ....

pm ....

You are now happy in the company of others who in turn are pleased to have you around. You benefit from being on the same mental wavelength as colleagues and new ideas coming from your direction can find their support readily. Some confusion over deeper, more personal relationships, could reign as the day wears on.

26 FRIDAY
Moon Age Day 9 ‹ Moon Sign Leo

am ....

pm ....

In a period of almost daily changes, you now find yourself shunning the limelight and making the most of your own company. Virgo does go through quiet spells. so your friends may not be too surprised at the way you are behaving. It would still be sensible to explain yourself fully if you get the chance.

27 SATURDAY
Moon Age Day 10 ‹ Moon Sign Leo

am ....

pm ....

Do not be surprised if some of your ideas or opinions seem to be unusual or radical when viewed through the eyes of others. The reason is that you have a much wider angle of vision than the world at large at present, but even so try not to alienate those who have a more conservative view of life than you do at present.

28 SUNDAY
Moon Age Day 11 ‹ Moon Sign Virgo

am ....

pm ....

The Moon comes full circle and turns up again in the sign of Virgo. Probably the most potent aid to success this month, the present trends tend to galvanise you into the sort of actions which you have thought about earlier, but never really got round to. Natural support comes from people who recognise your mood.

← NEGATIVE TREND							POSITIVE TREND →				
-5	-4	-3	-2	-1			+1	+2	+3	+4	+5
					LOVE						
					MONEY						
					LUCK						
					VITALITY						

29 MONDAY
Moon Age Day 12 ‹ Moon Sign Virgo

am ....

pm ....

Probably a day of significant good luck, though present trends being what they are, it might be necessary to curb your enthusiasms a little and simply accept the positive trends that life itself places around you. In social situations you tend to be very entertaining and are popular with many people.

30 TUESDAY
Moon Age Day 13 ‹ Moon Sign Virgo

am ....

pm ....

It looks as though present associations in your chart at present are inclined to make you rather more stubborn than would normally even be the case even for Virgo. It seems as if others are deliberately setting themselves up against you, though the truth is that you are not viewing life fairly yourself.

1 WEDNESDAY
Moon Age Day 14 ‹ Moon Sign Libra

am ....

pm ....

After the absolute tendency to follow your own path yesterday, the pendulum swings yet again and you now find yourself in a much calmer and more cooperative frame of mind. Things change so quickly at present that you might even make yourself dizzy with the potentials. Take time out to reflect on your life.

2 THURSDAY
Moon Age Day 15 ‹ Moon Sign Libra

am ....

pm ....

Though relationships seem to be going well enough, you could feel some slight dissatisfaction because you are over-emphasizing the glamour aspects of love and relationships. Of course, other people have their point of view, which it has to be said you may not be seeing as clearly at present as might normally be the case.

3 FRIDAY
Moon Age Day 16 ‹ Moon Sign Scorpio

am ....

pm ....

Although social pursuits and get-togethers offer the opportunity of much needed light relief, you could be brooding about something that has come from the direction of a friend, or a group member. The most advantageous situation would be to talk things through and to allow others to know how you feel about situations.

4 SATURDAY
Moon Age Day 17 ‹ Moon Sign Scorpio

am ....

pm ....

The first weekend of the month sees another return to positive thinking and forms the best time to put requests to those who are in a position to be of real help to your plans and schemes. The more you can get such people on your side the better. Many Virgoans will also find themselves achieving a physical peak round about now.

5 SUNDAY
Moon Age Day 18 ‹ Moon Sign Sagittarius

am ....

pm ....

Happiness plays a large part in the running of the day. You could also be very captivated by the thought of freedom, the great outdoors, fresh fields and pastures new. It does appear that fate is trying to steer you in a more positive direction and you could do worse than listen to the little voice at the back of your mind that advises you.

← *NEGATIVE TREND*   *POSITIVE TREND* →

-5	-4	-3	-2	-1			+1	+2	+3	+4	+5
					LOVE						
					MONEY						
					LUCK						
					VITALITY						

1996

YOUR MONTH AT A GLANCE

The twelve numbered boxes represent the important areas in your life. The key to the numbers you will find beneath the panel. A Sun above the number indicates that opportunities are around. A Cloud below the number, that you should be a bit defensive. Nothing above or below and life will be pretty ordinary.

1	2	3	4	5	6	7	8	9	10	11	12

KEY

1 Strength of Personality
2 Personal Finance
3 Useful Information Gathering
4 Domestic Affairs
5 Pleasure & Romance
6 Effective Work & Health

7 One to One Relationships
8 Questioning, Thinking & Deciding
9 External Influences / Education
10 Career Aspirations
11 Teamwork Activities
12 Unconscious Impulses

MAY HIGHS AND LOWS

Here, I show how the rhythm of the Moon will affect you this month. Like the tide, your energies and abilities will rise and fall with its pattern. When it is above the date line, go-for-it. When it is below the line you should be resting.

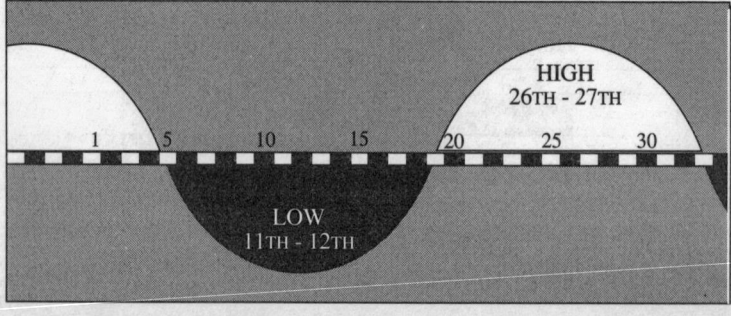

6 MONDAY   *Moon Age Day 19 • Moon Sign Sagittarius*

am ....

pm ....

The Sun is so strong now in your solar ninth house that it is important for you to to take opportunities when they arise, or to create them when they do not. The possibilities are now all in your own hands, and you won't find the world looking out for you, unless you take something of a hand in the situation yourself.

7 TUESDAY   *Moon Age Day 20 • Moon Sign Capricorn*

am ....

pm ....

If a change of direction seems providential now, with everything on your side you can afford to take the chance. Issues surrounding finance can easily raise doubts in your mind, but you must condition yourself not to over-react. Check all details carefully before you commit yourself to any particular course of action.

8 WEDNESDAY   *Moon Age Day 21 • Moon Sign Capricorn*

am ....

pm ....

The light of life shines positively on all matters associated with love and enjoyment. You now look for both in equal quantity and do your best to make situations comfortable for others, as well as for yourself. Enterprise and enthusiasm are not really in doubt, and neither is your ability to use them properly.

9 THURSDAY   *Moon Age Day 22 • Moon Sign Aquarius*

am ....

pm ....

The secrets that others divulge to you today, especially in a professional sense, are not to be relied upon completely. All details require double checking and relaxation only comes with the social aspects at the end of the day. Practical jokes are not to your liking now and you are likely to tell people so.

10 FRIDAY
Moon Age Day 23 ‹ Moon Sign Aquarius

am ....

pm ....

Don't wait around for a suitable moment for anything today. Instead of doing so, take each minute for what it is worth and do what you know to be right. Following your intuition, even though it is usually strong, is not all that easy for you, but you really have to try and do so just now, and it is possible.

11 SATURDAY
Moon Age Day 24 ‹ Moon Sign Pisces

am ....

pm ....

The Virgoan bossy-boots now puts in an appearance and shows you to be assuming an assertive, authoritative role. This is especially evident at home, when domestic affairs are probably not helped by your constant interference. You can be a real help to other people now, but not if you are constantly telling them what to do.

12 SUNDAY
Moon Age Day 25 ‹ Moon Sign Pisces

am ....

pm ....

Things are not particularly good at the moment, and once again it is down to a combination of the Moon, which is in your opposite sign, and very changeable aspects in your chart that are firing off all the time. Sit still and watch life go by, without fussing, without worrying and in the knowledge that all is well.

	NEGATIVE TREND							POSITIVE TREND			
-5	-4	-3	-2	-1			+1	+2	+3	+4	+5
					LOVE						
					MONEY						
					LUCK						
					VITALITY						

13 MONDAY
Moon Age Day 26 ‹ Moon Sign Pisces

am ....

pm ....

Competitive career moves become possible as a result of news received now. In the main it would be sensible to keep to tried and tested methods of getting things done, despite the fact that you have new ideas up your sleeve. Progress is made generally easier by the practical help coming in from new directions.

14 TUESDAY
Moon Age Day 27 ‹ Moon Sign Aries

am ....

pm ....

You could easily find yourself restless for fresh fields and pastures new. Although at times such trends can be seen as negative, this is certainly not the case now. You have to make things turn out the way you want them to in your heart, and not necessarily in your head. Right now you have the power to do so.

15 WEDNESDAY
Moon Age Day 28 ‹ Moon Sign Aries

am ....

pm ....

A friendly attitude to one and all stands you in good stead when it comes to other people noticing you. Unexpected social invitations are worth a second look and even strangers show more than a passing interest in you now. Conforming to expected patterns can be rather difficult but proves advantageous later.

16 THURSDAY
Moon Age Day 29 ‹ Moon Sign Taurus

am ....

pm ....

Avoid the temptation to play 'Devils's advocate' in other people's arguments today. It would be far better sticking to what you know personally and staying away from situations that do not really involve you at all. Perhaps you do not have quite the same amount of determinations as has been the case recently.

17 FRIDAY

Moon Age Day 0 ‹ Moon Sign Taurus

am ....

pm ....

Now is a time to be on good terms with just about everyone you come across, and of course this could turn out to be a very positive thing. Because you are very popular, there are potential gains to be made that you haven't even thought about recently, so it is very important that you remain flexible.

18 SATURDAY

Moon Age Day 1 ‹ Moon Sign Gemini

am ....

pm ....

It is fairly rare that your natural attitude would give offence to other people, but you are not the best diplomat in the zodiac all the same. You can have days when it would be best to keep quiet rather than to give offence. In some ways, this is such a day, though more in casual rather than personal situations.

19 SUNDAY

Moon Age Day 2 ‹ Moon Sign Gemini

am ....

pm ....

In a financial sense, you now show a tendency to go to extremes, something that you would probably avoid if you took the trouble to think things through correctly. There is some useful advice about in a more personal sense, though you might find it hard to listen to contrary opinions at present.

← NEGATIVE TREND							POSITIVE TREND →			
-5	-4	-3	-2	-1		+1	+2	+3	+4	+5
					LOVE					
					MONEY					
					LUCK					
					VITALITY					

20 MONDAY
Moon Age Day 3 ‹ Moon Sign Gemini

am ....

pm ....

Another potentially good day, and this one responsive to your need to socialise with others. Give and take are very important, and for today at least, are not difficult to find in yourself. Creating more space around you at home could also be a good diversion, and prove to be of great significance later.

21 TUESDAY
Moon Age Day 4 ‹ Moon Sign Cancer

am ....

pm ....

Attracting the help of friends and acquaintances is easy, even if outsiders are not so simple to come to terms with. This would not be an ideal period for deciding to go it alone work-wise, and co-operation works wonders. A very chatty Virgoan greets the day, making all communication with others easy.

22 WEDNESDAY
Moon Age Day 5 ‹ Moon Sign Cancer

am ....

pm ....

If anyone decides to start arguments today, it would be much better if it wasn't you personally. You cannot really gain anything through pushing yourself too hard and this, in itself, may also lead to a short temper. You will only kick yourself later on if you allow your antagonism to show now.

23 THURSDAY
Moon Age Day 6 ‹ Moon Sign Leo

am ....

pm ....

You cannot prepare for every eventuality that life may throw in your path, though you are looking ahead very well at present and should be able to arrange things better than even you expect. Together with your friends you are able to put new incentives into operation, which could mean a little excitement.

24 FRIDAY
Moon Age Day 7 ‹ Moon Sign Leo

am ....

pm ....

Beware of expecting too much of loved ones, who may not be in the best possible situation to do you any favours at present. The point is that it may not be their fault, so judging too harshly is also a mistake. Meanwhile, you end the working week on a fairly high note and can make the most of some chance encounters.

25 SATURDAY
Moon Age Day 8 ‹ Moon Sign Leo

am ....

pm ....

Professional matters are almost certainly at rest, as Virgoans settle into what should be an interesting and positive sort of weekend. No matter how many other issues may cross your mind at present, the most important factor is your social life. Now is a time to shine out in company and to make heads turn.

26 SUNDAY
Moon Age Day 9 ‹ Moon Sign Virgo

am ....

pm ....

The lunar high is of use to you now and you find that you are embarking on a significant winning streak in many spheres of your life. Probably the only potential problem is taking on more than you know to be good for you. This could be especially evident at home, where you may try to sort everything out on this Sunday.

← NEGATIVE TREND						POSITIVE TREND →				
-5	-4	-3	-2	-1		+1	+2	+3	+4	+5
					LOVE					
					MONEY					
					LUCK					
					VITALITY					

27 MONDAY   *Moon Age Day 10 ‹ Moon Sign Virgo*

am ....

pm ....

The Moon hangs around in your sign, bringing grace and favour
from a number of different directions, together with significant good
luck at the start of this working week. Make the most of favourable
chances that occur and bear in mind that there are times when life
itself turns out to be your best advisor.

28 TUESDAY   *Moon Age Day 11 ‹ Moon Sign Libra*

am ....

pm ....

You occupy an important position as far as family matters are
concerned, so that others are taking more notice of you than you
would normally give yourself credit for. The truth is that you play
more of a part in the decision making of people generally than you
are willing to believe, which is quite a responsibility.

29 WEDNESDAY   *Moon Age Day 12 ‹ Moon Sign Libra*

am ....

pm ....

You should find any sort of mental challenge or debate to be of
significant interest at this time, even though these could turn into
genuine disputes if others have their way. Mars is in your solar
ninth house, bringing extra determination and a desire to win that,
for the moment, sets your sign well and truly apart.

30 THURSDAY   *Moon Age Day 13 ‹ Moon Sign Scorpio*

am ....

pm ....

In situations where you know that others are more knowledgeable
than you are it would be a good idea to defer to their choices. This is
a period when too many cooks definitely could spoil the broth, not a
situation that would prove to be very helpful in the fullness of time.
Patience is hard to maintain.

31 FRIDAY
Moon Age Day 14 ‹ Moon Sign Scorpio

am ....

pm ....

Socially speaking there are likely to be some people who you just can't manage to get along with, no matter how much you try to do so. Intimate relationships are a different matter altogether however and respond well to your romantic and very positive approach. A good day for receiving and giving compliments.

1 SATURDAY
Moon Age Day 15 ‹ Moon Sign Scorpio

am ....

pm ....

The spotlight is now on domestic matters and the way that you are prepared to deal with them. You are not really in any danger of treading on the toes of others and should find yourself to be far more understanding now than would occasionally be the case. Rewards at home are of a personal nature and are very welcome.

2 SUNDAY
Moon Age Day 16 ‹ Moon Sign Sagittarius

am ....

pm ....

Mare is still figuring strongly in your chart, stimulating a number of important debates and gradually making you more dynamic in your approach to life than would often be the case. Today you become much more competitive in your associations with others, not somethng that they can come to terms with unless you talk to them.

← *NEGATIVE TREND*　　　　　　　　*POSITIVE TREND* →

-5	-4	-3	-2	-1		+1	+2	+3	+4	+5
					LOVE					
					MONEY					
					LUCK					
					VITALITY					

1996

YOUR MONTH AT A GLANCE

The twelve numbered boxes represent the important areas in your life. The key to the numbers you will find beneath the panel. A Sun above the number indicates that opportunities are around. A Cloud below the number, that you should be a bit defensive. Nothing above or below and life will be pretty ordinary.

		☀		☀		☀					
1	2	3	4	5	6	7	8	9	10	11	12
								☁	☁		

KEY

1 Strength of Personality
2 Personal Finance
3 Useful Information Gathering
4 Domestic Affairs
5 Pleasure & Romance
6 Effective Work & Health
7 One to One Relationships
8 Questioning, Thinking & Deciding
9 External Influences / Education
10 Career Aspirations
11 Teamwork Activities
12 Unconscious Impulses

JUNE HIGHS AND LOWS

Here, I show how the rhythm of the Moon will affect you this month. Like the tide, your energies and abilities will rise and fall with its pattern. When it is above the date line, go-for-it. When it is below the line you should be resting.

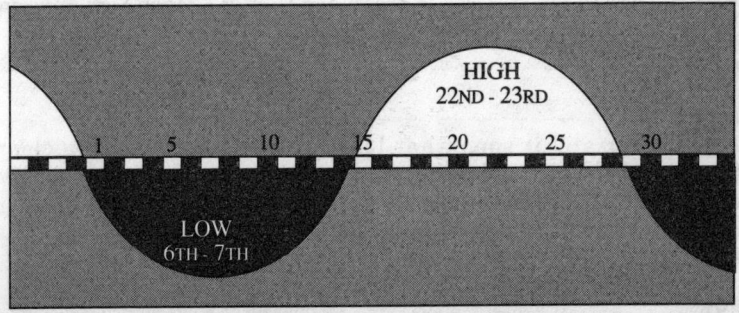

3 MONDAY
Moon Age Day 17 • Moon Sign Sagittarius

am ....

pm ....

Though your mind works well and quickly at the start of this working week, be very careful that you do not speak in haste. There is every chance that you will regret the fact later and it would be far better not to allow the situation to occur in the first place. Some friends could prove to be very helpful.

4 TUESDAY
Moon Age Day 18• Moon Sign Capricorn

am ....

pm ....

There is still a competitive edge to you, but for the remainder of the week this could turn out to be a good thing. Others will hold you in greater respect than they have previously, as long as your point of view is rational and sensible. For this reason, and others, you won't expect second best from yourself or others.

5 WEDNESDAY
Moon Age Day 19 • Moon Sign Capricorn

am ....

pm ....

Although you have a tendency to speak first and think about the consequences later just at the moment, you also have enough cheek and sufficient diplomacy to get you out of any potential difficulty as a result. You are looking for new and exciting possibilities in your life, even if friends have other plans.

6 THURSDAY
Moon Age Day 20 • Moon Sign Aquarius

am ....

pm ....

An appropriate, it somewhat late, time to have a spring clean, though this will probably not extend to the way you live domestically. It is your mind that receives the attention and you are now determined to leave behind ideas and stumbling blocks that have proved difficult before. Many new incentives come along.

7 FRIDAY

Moon Age Day 21 ‹ Moon Sign Aquarius

am ....

pm ....

Resist the urge to dwell on the past, because although certain aspects of it do seem to find you out on a number of occasions today, to worry about it really would not be much use. In some respects you will be doing all that you can to maintain a low-profile at present, which could come as a surprise to others.

8 SATURDAY

Moon Age Day 22 ‹ Moon Sign Pisces

am ....

pm ....

It would be best to maintain a rather low profile just for the moment. The lunar low should not be too difficult to deal with this time round, though it could still stop you in your tracks concerning projects and ideas that are close to your heart. Negative moods become slightly more likely than usual.

9 SUNDAY

Moon Age Day 23 ‹ Moon Sign Pisces

am ....

pm ....

Some of your personal choices may be limited right now, which is why you are more likely to get on with matters that you already know and understand, instead of trying to break too much in the way of new ground. All the same, the day should be happy and does leave you the time to get a little relaxation into your life.

← *NEGATIVE TREND*   *POSITIVE TREND* →

-5	-4	-3	-2	-1			+1	+2	+3	+4	+5
					LOVE						
					MONEY						
					LUCK						
					VITALITY						

10 MONDAY
Moon Age Day 24 ‹ Moon Sign Aries

am ....

pm ....

The Sun is in your solar tenth house, and you see one or two potential professional successes coming along as a result. You do need change in your life, so staying around in the same place too long does not really appeal to you at all for the moment. When dealing with loved ones, attitudes are all important.

11 TUESDAY
Moon Age Day 25 ‹ Moon Sign Aries

am ....

pm ....

A day of fairly unusual happenings and possibly one or two dramatic encounters too. This would not be a good interlude for taking chances financially, so preserve your hard-earned cash as much as you can for the moment. Look carefully at relationships that may have been going wrong recently.

12 WEDNESDAY
Moon Age Day 26 ‹ Moon Sign Taurus

am ....

pm ....

Try to get a feeling of variety in your life. This has been an important consideration all month, but is especially significant right now. Although it might seem at first that not everyone has your best interests at heart, it won't be long before you realise that there is much goodness in those around you. You simply fail to see it.

13 THURSDAY
Moon Age Day 23 ‹ Moon Sign Capricorn

am ....

pm ....

Most meetings, appointments and travel arrangements go according to plan and this should not be a day when life is throwing any sort of obstacle in your path. Any journey that you do make today probably won't be especially long in terms of duration, though you do not have to go far now to enjoy yourself.

14 FRIDAY

Moon Age Day 28 ‹ Moon Sign Taurus

am ....

pm ....

If any sort of professional proposition is put to you today, it might be worth looking at it very carefully before you dismiss it out of hand. In most areas of your life you could be rather too impulsive for once, a fact that could work against your best interests in the end. All the same, sit back and enjoy the journey of life.

15 SATURDAY

Moon Age Day 0 ‹ Moon Sign Gemini

am ....

pm ....

The needs of the day from a practical point of view look like interfering with what should also be an important social interlude. It would be sensible to look at all situations carefully before proceeding. You may be taking on a number of responsibilities that have little to do with you personally.

16 SUNDAY

Moon Age Day 1 ‹ Moon Sign Gemini

am ....

pm ....

You now have four planets sitting in your solar tenth house. One result of this fact seems to be that the more humble you show yourself to be in any given situation, the more likely it is that you will gain as a result. Creative responses are good for the weekend, and any travel could well lead to new interests.

← *NEGATIVE TREND*							*POSITIVE TREND* →			
-5	-4	-3	-2	-1		+1	+2	+3	+4	+5
					LOVE					
					MONEY					
					LUCK					
					VITALITY					

17 MONDAY

Moon Age Day 2 ‹ Moon Sign Cancer

am ....

pm ....

A combination of planetary aspects on this Monday make you decide that your ideas are not so strange after all. In fact almost anything is worth a second look now, in contrast to last week when you were more inclined to find value in ideas from outside. Convincing others that you are correct may not be too easy.

18 TUESDAY

Moon Age Day 3 ‹ Moon Sign Cancer

am ....

pm ....

Career prospects, as well as your desire to succeed in other matters, could be hampered by the unintentional actions of those around you. Don't hold this fact against them because it does look as though others have a strong desire to help you out if they can. A time to exhibit more than a little patience.

19 WEDNESDAY

Moon Age Day 4 ‹ Moon Sign Leo

am ....

pm ....

There is a positive focus on money-matters and a need to sort out today's complications before you move on to any for the future. The people in your immediate vicinity seem more than willing to settle for what you believe, even if they have different ideas themselves. Officials could be very demanding.

20 THURSDAY

Moon Age Day 5 ‹ Moon Sign Leo

am ....

pm ....

Fun, in all its forms, is there for the taking today. It seems as though the whole world comes to its door to wave as you pass right now and the carefree side of Virgo that this creates is a particularly good sight to see. Information coming in tends to indicate that your influence upon others is on the increase.

21 FRIDAY

Moon Age Day 6 ‹ Moon Sign Virgo

am ....

pm ....

There is a busy atmosphere around, so much so that it is very unlikely that you would get through everything that is of importance to you just at present. Priorities need to be sorted out as quickly as possible because you do need some sort of routine to work towards. Personal frustrations can be resolved.

22 SATURDAY

Moon Age Day 7 ‹ Moon Sign Virgo

am ....

pm ....

Now more interested than ever to know what makes other people tick, do what you can to help out but avoid becoming involved in the complicated lives of people who you will never really be able to understand. High spirits are in evidence and leisure interests could predominate, especially later in the day.

23 SUNDAY

Moon Age Day 8 ‹ Moon Sign Libra

am ....

pm ....

Once again the Moon comes good for you as it sails majestically into your own sign of Virgo. Happy and carefree, you enjoy what Sunday has to offer in itself, whilst at the same time keeping one eye firmly on the week that stands before you. A mixture of work and play turns out to be a cocktail that you cannot resist.

← *NEGATIVE TREND*							*POSITIVE TREND* →			
-5	-4	-3	-2	-1		+1	+2	+3	+4	+5
					LOVE					
					MONEY					
					LUCK					
					VITALITY					

24 MONDAY

Moon Age Day 9 ‹ Moon Sign Libra

am ....

pm ....

Some important career moves may not be all that far away now and it would be worth looking at the options carefully before you allow yourself to make any irrevocable decision. In terms of popularity you should now be reaching a peak and can even have a good talk to people who do not usually understand you.

25 TUESDAY

Moon Age Day 10 ‹ Moon Sign Libra

am ....

pm ....

You should be able to strike a happy medium now between catering for the needs that your nearest and dearest have of you and also fulfilling your expectations of yourself professionally. A friend may be invaluable when it comes to offering you just the right advice at the correct moment.

26 WEDNESDAY

Moon Age Day 11 ‹ Moon Sign Scorpio

am ....

pm ....

It's hard to make everything work out exactly the way that you would wish it to do right now, and the secret probably is not to try. Life jogs along well enough as long as you resist the urge to interfere with it, something that all air sign people find difficult. Friends have good reasons for their behaviour.

27 THURSDAY

Moon Age Day 12 ‹ Moon Sign Scorpio

am ....

pm ....

Where important personal decisions are concerned, it would be a good idea to defer some of them until a little later, even though these may be issues that crop up time and again. In a financial sense there may be a need for some cutbacks, even if these are only temporary. Do what you must.

28 FRIDAY

Moon Age Day 13 ‹ Moon Sign Sagittarius

am ....

pm ....

Friday proves to be just a little problematic, if only because your discover that much of your attention is being turned back towards the needs and wants that people at home have of you. Finding the right sort of balance may not be especially easy today, but it is very necessary.

29 SATURDAY

Moon Age Day 14 ‹ Moon Sign Sagittarius

am ....

pm ....

Not a good period for building up your hopes in practical matters, though an excellent time for planning rather than doing. Contradictions in the behaviour of those around you could have more to do with the way that you are looking at life than they do with reality. Try to take an impartial point-of-view if you can.

30 SUNDAY

Moon Age Day 15 ‹ Moon Sign Sagittarius

am ....

pm ....

You can have a real calming influence on the people you live with now, in direct contradiction to some of the possible happenings of yesterday. The reason is a series of positive aspect now emerging in your solar chart. Money matters show considerable improvement, even if you have to wait a while for it.

← NEGATIVE TREND						POSITIVE TREND →				
-5	-4	-3	-2	-1		+1	+2	+3	+4	+5
					LOVE					
					MONEY					
					LUCK					
					VITALITY					

1996

YOUR MONTH AT A GLANCE

The twelve numbered boxes represent the important areas in your life. The key to the numbers you will find beneath the panel. A Sun above the number indicates that opportunities are around. A Cloud below the number, that you should be a bit defensive. Nothing above or below and life will be pretty ordinary.

1	2	3	4	5	6	7	8	9	10	11	12

KEY

1 Strength of Personality	7 One to One Relationships
2 Personal Finance	8 Questioning, Thinking & Deciding
3 Useful Information Gathering	9 External Influences / Education
4 Domestic Affairs	10 Career Aspirations
5 Pleasure & Romance	11 Teamwork Activities
6 Effective Work & Health	12 Unconscious Impulses

JULY HIGHS AND LOWS

Here, I show how the rhythm of the Moon will affect you this month. Like the tide, your energies and abilities will rise and fall with its pattern. When it is above the date line, go-for-it. When it is below the line you should be resting.

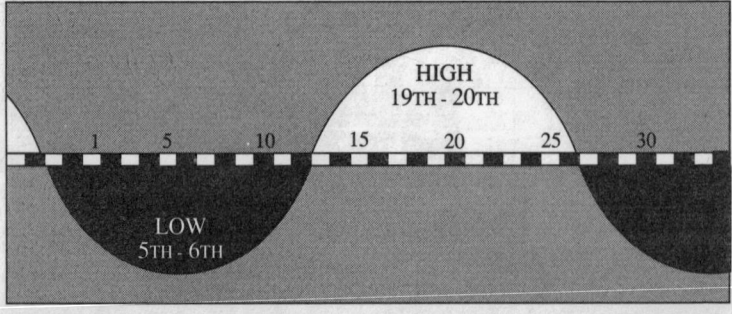

1 MONDAY

Moon Age Day 16 • Moon Sign Capricorn

am ....

pm ....

A time to be keeping your ego firmly in check because you are inclined to go over the top otherwise. Not everyone understands you as well as your nearest and dearest to, so it's particularly important to make a favourable impression on strangers. Confidence grows with the day, and you feel ready for anything.

2 TUESDAY

Moon Age Day 17 • Moon Sign Capricorn

am ....

pm ....

It could appear that others are in a particularly argumentative mood today, so you may have to show a little more patience than would normally be the case. Keep an open mind about changes that become necessary in the family and be on hand to help out with any slight difficulties that arise.

3 WEDNESDAY

Moon Age Day 18 • Moon Sign Aquarius

am ....

pm ....

A loved one should now be playing a more dominant role in your life, and its true that those people close to you do have some interesting facts and figures to reveal. Professionally speaking, this could be a good time to seek out the support and advice of an expert, especially regarding changes to working routines.

4 THURSDAY

Moon Age Day 19 • Moon Sign Aquarius

am ....

pm ....

The Sun is now strong in your solar eleventh house, so don't be too surprised if you find that friends and relatives alike turn out to be extremely anxious to put themselves out on your behalf. This could be an invaluable trend, and one that you should look at very carefully. A little assistance now goes a long way.

5 FRIDAY   *Moon Age Day 20 ‹ Moon Sign Pisces*

am ....

pm ....

Because the lunar low now comes along, you should not be too
surprised to discover that you are in a rather less ambitious mood
than may have been the case for the last couple of days. New
incentives do arrive too, though it is not especially likely that you
would be picking up on them for the moment.

6 SATURDAY   *Moon Age Day 21 ‹ Moon Sign Pisces*

am ....

pm ....

Pressing obligations of one sort or another could be taking up the
greatest percentage of your day, though you should do your best to
find time for people close to home who are relying on you
significantly at this time. Look out for a pleasant surprise or two
later in the day.

7 SUNDAY   *Moon Age Day 22 ‹ Moon Sign Aries*

am ....

pm ....

Laid-back and even lazy tendencies are the order of the day, and
why not, this is Sunday after all? If you have the chance do only
those things that take your fancy, do not be held back from any sort
of venture simply because one or two people around you do not think
that your ideas are sound.

← NEGATIVE TREND								POSITIVE TREND →			
-5	-4	-3	-2	-1			+1	+2	+3	+4	+5
					LOVE						
					MONEY						
					LUCK						
					VITALITY						

8 MONDAY   *Moon Age Day 23 ‹ Moon Sign Aries*

am ....

pm ....

Although today should be set fair for a number of successes, it is also possible that you could get on the wrong side of certain people who could be of great assistance to you. There is really no point in creating opponents at all today, so be as tactful as you are able and use practical skills in conjunction with your intuition.

9 TUESDAY   *Moon Age Day 24 ‹ Moon Sign Taurus*

am ....

pm ....

There are great rewards coming from the direction of family members today and this is the direction in which your mind is likely to turn. Not that this means you have abandoned efforts in a more practical direction, though it is possible that one or two ideas will have to be shelved for the moment.

10 WEDNESDAY   *Moon Age Day 25 ‹ Moon Sign Taurus*

am ....

pm ....

If others try to dampen your enthusiasm it is especially important to make certain that they do not get the chance. Trying to please everyone could be practically impossible and you could be left with the feeling that you would be better off simply doing whatever takes your personal fancy for now.

11 THURSDAY   *Moon Age Day 26 ‹ Moon Sign Taurus*

am ....

pm ....

Fresh plans and the fulfilment of ambitions now stand out as being uppermost in your mind. What is more, there are options around that you may hardly have come to expect but which are likely to work well in your favour. Short-term plans are given a boost, thanks to the intervention of very positive types.

12 FRIDAY

Moon Age Day 27 ‹ Moon Sign Gemini

am ....

pm ....

There is a good chance that you will be displaying your friendliness to practically everyone you come across today. What you do for others can bring significant gains into your own life too and no effort seems to be wasted just at present. Some of the chances that come your way today are most unexpected.

13 SATURDAY

Moon Age Day 28 ‹ Moon Sign Gemini

am ....

pm ....

There are some obstacles to be overcome, and this is not necessarily a bad thing because it breeds a stronger sense of commitment to get on and act as you see fit. Much of what you accomplish today turns out to he highly satisfactory and sees you meeting challenges head-on. Leave some time for leisure.

14 SUNDAY

Moon Age Day 29 ‹ Moon Sign Cancer

am ....

pm ....

It might benefit you to maintain a slightly lower profile today than has been the case for the last day or two, especially if you have things on your mind and want an hour or two to yourself. All the same, don't allow yourself to give in easily when there are personal considerations to be dealt with.

← NEGATIVE TREND							POSITIVE TREND →			
-5	-4	-3	-2	-1		+1	+2	+3	+4	+5
					LOVE					
					MONEY					
					LUCK					
					VITALITY					

15 MONDAY   *Moon Age Day 0 ‹ Moon Sign Cancer*

am ....

pm ....

A sombre atmosphere should be dealt with as soon as proves to
practical, probably by turning on the charm and trying to lighten
things up a little. An oversight on the part of others could bring one
or two complications into your own life, especially with regard to
travel or change of any sort.

16 TUESDAY   *Moon Age Day 1 ‹ Moon Sign Cancer*

am ....

pm ....

Someone not too far from you in a personal or social sense seems to
be doing all that they can to dampen your enthusiasm for life.
Sometimes you can take things for granted and would be advised at
present to look at relationships and what you may be able to do in
order to straighten them out a little.

17 WEDNESDAY   *Moon Age Day 2 ‹ Moon Sign Leo*

am ....

pm ....

Romance begins to stimulate the more idealistic qualities within
your nature and makes it important that you say all the things that
are on your mind, perhaps even if you are not really certain what
sort of a response you are likely to receive. In a more practical sense
a healthy scepticism would seem wise.

18 THURSDAY   *Moon Age Day 3 ‹ Moon Sign Leo*

am ....

pm ....

Past emotional issues that still play on your mind should be sorted
out as soon as it proves to be possible. The last thing that you need
right now is gremlins from the past throwing a spanner in the works
of your present life. All the same, sometimes things just have to be
dealt with, and now is a good time for doing so.

19 FRIDAY

Moon Age Day 4 ‹ Moon Sign Virgo

am ....

pm ....

The lunar high comes along, and the presence of the Moon in your own sign turns out to be especially useful practically speaking. Now is the time to put all plans into action and to get on with jobs that you may have been putting off for a while. Friends can be very helpful and will offer the sort of practical assistance you need.

20 SATURDAY

Moon Age Day 5 ‹ Moon Sign Virgo

am ....

pm ....

It looks as thought you can now get others to see things your own way, without having to argue with them. The really friendly side of your nature begins to display itself, offering you a strong social aspect to the day. The only negative trend could be that you do not feel like doing anything that goes against the grain personally.

21 SUNDAY

Moon Age Day 6 ‹ Moon Sign Virgo

am ....

pm ....

The Sun now stands strongly in your solar eleventh house and you are able to gain the help and support of all kinds of people. This is a trend that continues for the next month or so, and you can make particular gains because others are so willing to put themselves out on your behalf. You probably feel very secure at this time.

← *NEGATIVE TREND*   *POSITIVE TREND* →

-5	-4	-3	-2	-1		+1	+2	+3	+4	+5
					LOVE					
					MONEY					
					LUCK					
					VITALITY					

22 MONDAY
Moon Age Day 7 ‹ Moon Sign Libra

am ....

pm ....

If there is any spare time on your hands, you won't have much trouble finding a use for it. Personal progress is now made less difficult with the added advantage of better financial prospects and people being willing to put themselves out on your behalf. Close relationships bring out the best in you.

23 TUESDAY
Moon Age Day 8 ‹ Moon Sign Libra

am ....

pm ....

This would be a good time to take a break, if to do so at short notice proves to be possible. You are in need of fresh fields and pastures new, and you will not want to put up with the wayward behaviour of certain people in your vicinity. It is important to let other people know how sincere you can be at present.

24 WEDNESDAY
Moon Age Day 9 ‹ Moon Sign Scorpio

am ....

pm ....

There are certain types around who are still doing their best to distract you from working to your best potential. As long as you remain positive in your attitude this will not be any sort of problem to you because, as always, you know better than anyone else what direction you want your life to be taking.

25 THURSDAY
Moon Age Day 10 ‹ Moon Sign Scorpio

am ....

pm ....

It should now be really easy to bring others round to your way of thinking. In social and personal discussions you will need to put your best foot forward and to make the most of any contacts of a useful nature that come your way. Minor financial gains can come as a result of some limited speculation.

26 FRIDAY
Moon Age Day 11 ‹ Moon Sign Sagittarius

am ....

pm ....

A special occasion could be beckoning at home, or with regard to the way friends are behaving. You tend to put the needs of others first today but should not try to follow routines too much. A little dose of individuality works to your advantage, and you have to stay away from tedious routines of any sort.

27 SATURDAY
Moon Age Day 12 ‹ Moon Sign Sagittarius

am ....

pm ....

There should be great cause for optimism all round today. With the weekend at your disposal, and plenty of personal options open, it is very important to push ahead with your own plans, and not to take too much notice of less positive types who impinge on your life. More than usual good luck becomes possible.

28 SUNDAY
Moon Age Day 13 ‹ Moon Sign Capricorn

am ....

pm ....

There is someone about who is trying to kid or bully you into doing things that may go against the grain personally. You are not easily intimidated however, and will opt to please yourself in the long-run. Find time to whisper words of love to the person who is most important to you, and who may be feeling neglected.

	-5	-4	-3	-2	-1		+1	+2	+3	+4	+5
LOVE											
MONEY											
LUCK											
VITALITY											

← *NEGATIVE TREND*   *POSITIVE TREND* →

29 MONDAY
Moon Age Day 14 ‹ Moon Sign Capricorn

am ....

pm ....

The news that comes in from family members and loved ones in general tends to be stimulating and to lift your spirits no end. This may be the best time of the month to be dealing with matters associated with house and home, though it is also important not to allow more professional matters to slide too much.

30 TUESDAY
Moon Age Day 15 ‹ Moon Sign Aquarius

am ....

pm ....

Significant conflict of interest now becomes obvious, as you try to juggle with the various needs that life puts upon you, both at work and at home. It is possible to keep things apart and yet working smoothly, even if it does take up much of your energy to do so. Please yourself whenever the mood takes you.

31 WEDNESDAY
Moon Age Day 16 ‹ Moon Sign Aquarius

am ....

pm ....

A time to put many of your new ideas into practice, no matter what your friends and associated may think about them. In a more personal sense, you can expect a warm reception from people who have your best interests at heart, and though in some way your confidence may not be too high, you can make great progress.

1 THURSDAY
Moon Age Day 17 ‹ Moon Sign Pisces

am ....

pm ....

The lunar low brings a temporary lull into your life, together with some enforced rest. It's really a case of being willing to note the patterns of life and not to be working against them, which would only lead to difficulties further down the line. Confidence may be lowered a little but is not stifled.

2 FRIDAY

Moon Age Day 18 ‹ Moon Sign Pisces

am ....

pm ....

Leave time for watching the flowers grow. Especially if the weather is good it would be great to get out and about at some stage today, and to really be yourself, freed from some of the fetters that everyday life places upon you. If others are surprised by your attitude, the situation may do them some good.

3 SATURDAY

Moon Age Day 19 ‹ Moon Sign Aries

am ....

pm ....

In a social sense you should now be in great demand. Don't underestimate your own popularity, especially in the company of people who carry genuine influence to change your life for the better. With the Sun now very important in your chart, you are seen in a very positive light by almost everyone you meet.

4 SUNDAY

Moon Age Day 20 ‹ Moon Sign Aries

am ....

pm ....

The casual remarks made by other people should not be seen as a challenge to your own authority, though the present state of your chart is inclined to make you see them in this way if you are not careful. A short argumentative streak is possible, though not if you find an hour or two to be on your own.

← NEGATIVE TREND   POSITIVE TREND →

-5	-4	-3	-2	-1		+1	+2	+3	+4	+5
					LOVE					
					MONEY					
					LUCK					
					VITALITY					

1996

YOUR MONTH AT A GLANCE

The twelve numbered boxes represent the important areas in your life.
The key to the numbers you will find beneath the panel. A Sun above
the number indicates that opportunities are around. A Cloud below
the number, that you should be a bit defensive. Nothing above or
below and life will be pretty ordinary.

1	2	3	4	5	6	7	8	9	10	11	12

KEY

1 Strength of Personality
2 Personal Finance
3 Useful Information Gathering
4 Domestic Affairs
5 Pleasure & Romance
6 Effective Work & Health

7 One to One Relationships
8 Questioning, Thinking & Deciding
9 External Influences / Education
10 Career Aspirations
11 Teamwork Activities
12 Unconscious Impulses

AUGUST HIGHS AND LOWS

Here, I show how the rhythm of the Moon will affect you this month.
Like the tide, your energies and abilities will rise and fall with its pattern. When it is above the date line, go-for-it. When it is below the
line you should be resting.

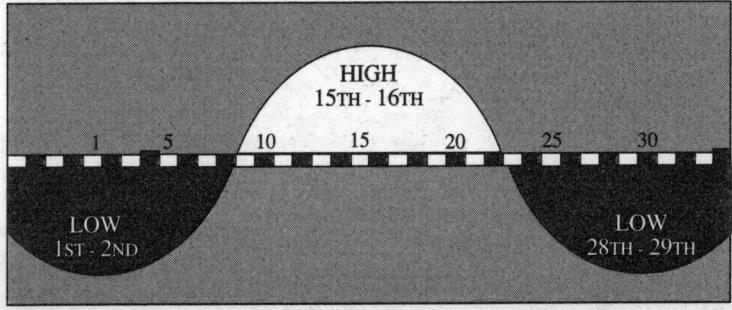

5 MONDAY
Moon Age Day 21 • Moon Sign Aries

am ....

pm ....

Your power of influence over others is especially well marked at the moment, but it is unlikely that you would use this trend in any selfish way. A busy start to the week makes it difficult for you to concentrate as much as you would wish on inconsequential details, though they have to be looked at eventually.

6 TUESDAY
Moon Age Day 22 • Moon Sign Taurus

am ....

pm ....

In a general and physical sense you could be at a low ebb. The secret is not to set yourself so many tasks that they cannot possibly be accomplished. Meanwhile other people are trying to load extra responsibilities upon you, a situation that you should try to avoid. It's time to recharge your batteries.

7 WEDNESDAY
Moon Age Day 23 • Moon Sign Taurus

am ....

pm ....

Confidence in your ideas comes from a host of different directions, a fact that makes for less cluttered horizons generally in the next few days. A very good time to be striking whilst the the iron is hot and not at all the sort of period when you should be holding back in any way. Don't be sparing with praise.

8 THURSDAY
Moon Age Day 24 • Moon Sign Gemini

am ....

pm ....

The long-term planning Virgoan is in evidence now. This brings the ability to look well ahead of yourself in matters of security and financial stability. Authority figures and employers are likely to be looking upon you favourably and situations at work turn to your advantage. Take charge of situations that other people find difficult.

9 FRIDAY
Moon Age Day 25 ‹ Moon Sign Geminir

am ....

pm ....

Your first concern for today is to keep ahead of new incentives and the sort of possibilities that crop up in your life all the time at present. In some senses you stand alone, because not everyone is in the same frame of mind as you are. Difficult situations can be put behind you relatively quickly.

10 SATURDAY
Moon Age Day 26 ‹ Moon Sign Cancer

am ....

pm ....

Communications skills are good and you have plenty to say for yourself at present. Of course this does not mean that everyone you come across wants to listen to what you have to say, but in the main you will get a fair hearing. Relatives and friends could cause you a worry or two, though probably not for long.

11 SUNDAY
Moon Age Day 27 ‹ Moon Sign Cancer

am ....

pm ....

For once you have it in your mind that your own needs outweigh those of the people you live with. Although this could be seen as being a fairly selfish attitude, in the end you manage to help everyone else too. Arguments are less than likely now because you have the ability to explain yourself without causing offence.

← *NEGATIVE TREND*   *POSITIVE TREND* →

-5	-4	-3	-2	-1		+1	+2	+3	+4	+5
					LOVE					
					MONEY					
					LUCK					
					VITALITY					

12 MONDAY

Moon Age Day 28 ‹ Moon Sign Cancer

am ....

pm ....

What you hear from colleagues and friends at the start of this working week may not be entirely true, and so you need to take many comments with a rather large pinch of salt. An atmospheric sort of day in some respects, with your intuition working well and a determination to get to the heart of any important matter.

13 TUESDAY

Moon Age Day 29 ‹ Moon Sign Leo

am ....

pm ....

Those amongst you who have heard of 'Karma' will be pleased to know that you are bringing good karma to yourself today. It's what you do for others that really counts, mainly because you are asking for little or nothing in return. Issues from the past would be really easy for you to deal with at the present time.

14 WEDNESDAY

Moon Age Day 0 ‹ Moon Sign Leo

am ....

pm ....

Serious issues are dealt with instantly, whilst impossible ones will take just a little longer. You might find that you are more tired than usual and if so will need to take the odd hour or two out to rest and relax. This would not be a good time to be expecting too much of yourself, despite you apparent success.

15 THURSDAY

Moon Age Day 1 ‹ Moon Sign Leo

am ....

pm ....

Stand by for the lunar high, which is upon you today. Not only are you very reasonable in your dealings with the world at large, but coming back in your direction are a number of gains that you may not even have been expecting. Money matters ease and good luck should attend most of your endeavours around this time.

16 FRIDAY
Moon Age Day 2 ‹ Moon Sign Virgo

am ....

pm ....

Make the most of the present position of the Moon, while it is in a very good position to help you out. This is the sign of Virgo at its very best, anxious to help and on hand to do whatever is necessary in order to make a more comfortable life for everyone concerned. If difficulties do arise they are easily dealt with.

17 SATURDAY
Moon Age Day 3 ‹ Moon Sign Virgo

am ....

pm ....

Your sense of responsibility with regard to your partner can be called into question, but you should not be reluctant to deal with serious relationship topics at present. The ability to enjoy yourself fully this weekend can be slightly marred by self-doubts which probably have no justification in fact. Think about important jobs.

18 SUNDAY
Moon Age Day 4 ‹ Moon Sign Libra

am ....

pm ....

Not only are your ideas unusual now, but they are particularly surprising from the point of view of others. Retaining a sense of logic is important, since not everyone can follow some temporarily irrational aspects attending your sign. You can become carried away with wild schemes if you are not careful.

← *NEGATIVE TREND*   *POSITIVE TREND* →

-5	-4	-3	-2	-1		+1	+2	+3	+4	+5
					LOVE					
					MONEY					
					LUCK					
					VITALITY					

19 MONDAY
Moon Age Day 5 ‹ Moon Sign Libra

am ....

pm ....

You present an attractive face to the world as a whole, developing a
positive self image and reflecting it in your activities outside the
home. You may even find it possible to inspire others and could note
that you are reaching a mental peak, particularly in your
observation of life's most personal objectives.

20 TUESDAY
Moon Age Day 6 ‹ Moon Sign Scorpio

am ....

pm ....

Check carefully before you commit yourself to any appointment for
the future that you are not really sure about. This could be a good
day for carrying your diary around with you, since you are almost
certain to make mistakes otherwise. Still, these are not issues that
you should be taking all that seriously.

21 WEDNESDAY
Moon Age Day 7 ‹ Moon Sign Scorpio

am ....

pm ....

You have no worry now about owning up to your obligations, though
if you have problems from the past to resolve, make sure you are
realistic about your ability to sort things out. There are people
around who are only too willing to assist if you are not too proud to
listen. Professional decisions made now prove sensible.

22 THURSDAY
Moon Age Day 8 ‹ Moon Sign Scorpio

am ....

pm ....

If speculation is part of your nature, you stand more of a chance of
succeeding now that aspects favour taking a chance. General good
luck attends most spheres of your life, a situation that is assisted by
the fact that others are only too willing to let you have your own
way.

23 FRIDAY
Moon Age Day 9 ‹ Moon Sign Sagittarius

am ....

pm ....

A good way to end the working week, with a physical peak achieved and plenty of drive to spare. This does not mean that you should scatter your energies on too many different fronts but rather concentrate on specifics, together with the completion of tasks that are left over from past times.

24 SATURDAY
Moon Age Day 10 ‹ Moon Sign Sagittarius

am ....

pm ....

This could easily be a red letter day as far as your love life is concerned, so don't be at all surprised if romance comes your way at the moment. The attitude of friends can be a little difficult for you to understand, though probably not for long. You have enough intuition to know when others are about to let you down.

25 SUNDAY
Moon Age Day 11 ‹ Moon Sign Capricorn

am ....

pm ....

With the Sun now sitting in your solar first house, you look out towards a period of significantly greater personal rewards. These trends strike home right across the board and leave you feeling that just about anything your heart desires is now yours for the taking. Enterprise and enthusiasm now become the norm.

← *NEGATIVE TREND*   *POSITIVE TREND* →

-5	-4	-3	-2	-1		+1	+2	+3	+4	+5
					LOVE	▓				
					MONEY	▓				
			▓	▓	LUCK	▓				
					VITALITY	▓	▓	▓		

26 MONDAY
Moon Age Day 12 ‹ Moon Sign Capricorn

am ....

pm ....

All group involvements and team work activities are under the
spotlight now. The results of your own endeavours have improved
markedly, when co-operation is part of the scenario and you are
willing to seek the advice and support of those you work with. Later
in the day, do your best to keep close personal ties lighthearted.

27 TUESDAY
Moon Age Day 13 ‹ Moon Sign Aquarius

am ....

pm ....

The best physical and emotional peak of the month, with the Sun
doing much to support your plans and ideals, at a time when you
have so much going for you that it is difficult to know where to start.
Removing yourself from situations that you do not care for the look
of is as easy as pie for the sign of Virgo now.

28 WEDNESDAY
Moon Age Day 14 ‹ Moon Sign Aquarius

am ....

pm ....

Beware of extravagent tendencies in the middle of this week.
Despite the present generosity you show to friends and loved ones,
you ought to be counting the cost of life and perhaps drawing in your
horns a little. Those close to you can have some surprises,
particularly later in the day and this should make you happy.

29 THURSDAY
Moon Age Day 15 ‹ Moon Sign Pisces

am ....

pm ....

With a slight lack of self confidence regarding the way you approach
others, particularly influential figures, most of your ideas about
yourself need reframing due to an over active imagination. The
more cool and objective you manage to remain, the better life turns
in your direction. Contradictions are more or less inevitable.

30 FRIDAY

Moon Age Day 16 ‹ Moon Sign Pisces

am ....

pm ....

Associations in your solar chart today can go either way. That means there could be serious demands or a power struggle as a partner tries to dominate the proceedings, or alternatively that this is the role you take on yourself. In either case, circumstances require you to sit down and talk things through.

31 SATURDAY

Moon Age Day 17 ‹ Moon Sign Aries

am ....

pm ....

You seem very motivated by service and by doing what you can for other people today, yet surprisingly you are not in a particularly self-sacrificing mood. Strong intuitions come and go and need to be listened to carefully. Life generally is made easier as you begin to create rewards for yourself, almost without trying.

1 SUNDAY

Moon Age Day 18 ‹ Moon Sign Aries

am ....

pm ....

Much physical energy can be dissipated today, thanks to a conflict you notice within yourself. Pace yourself carefully and take on only one task at a time. It could feel as if you are living in another world, and as a result your imagination can play tricks on you. Not something to take too seriously.

← NEGATIVE TREND   POSITIVE TREND →

-5	-4	-3	-2	-1		+1	+2	+3	+4	+5
					LOVE					
					MONEY					
					LUCK					
					VITALITY					

1996

YOUR MONTH AT A GLANCE

The twelve numbered boxes represent the important areas in your life.
The key to the numbers you will find beneath the panel. A Sun above
the number indicates that opportunities are around. A Cloud below
the number, that you should be a bit defensive. Nothing above or
below and life will be pretty ordinary.

1	2	3 ☀	4	5 ☀	6	7 ☀	8	9	10	11	12
	☁								☁		

KEY

1 Strength of Personality
2 Personal Finance
3 Useful Information Gathering
4 Domestic Affairs
5 Pleasure & Romance
6 Effective Work & Health

7 One to One Relationships
8 Questioning, Thinking & Deciding
9 External Influences / Education
10 Career Aspirations
11 Teamwork Activities
12 Unconscious Impulses

SEPTEMBER HIGHS AND LOWS

Here, I show how the rhythm of the Moon will affect you this month.
Like the tide, your energies and abilities will rise and fall with its pattern. When it is above the date line, go-for-it. When it is below the
line you should be resting.

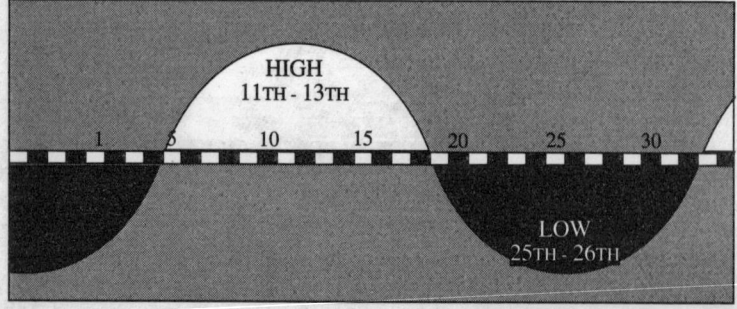

HIGH
11TH - 13TH

LOW
25TH - 26TH

2 MONDAY
Moon Age Day 19 • Moon Sign Aries

am ....

pm ....

Surprise visitors, phone calls and messages come rolling in as the week really get going, so at least you find yourself in excellent company. Minor successes come along in a professional field, if you are prepared to gamble. A satisfactory and productive time seems to be evident, but are you taking enough notice of it.

3 TUESDAY
Moon Age Day 20 • Moon Sign Taurus

am ....

pm ....

It would be best to avoid thinking that the grass may be greener on the other side of the fence because for today at least this is unlikely to be the case. The influence of both colleagues and friends could be rather pronounced at present, which is fine so long as their ideas make sense and they are being accommodating.

4 WEDNESDAY
Moon Age Day 21 • Moon Sign Taurus

am ....

pm ....

Combinations of aspects in your chart now indicate a preference at present for a number of casual contacts, with really close friends probably taking a back-seat in your life for a day or two. As far as your general life is concerned, it might be a good idea to think about yourself for once, doing what pleases you.

5 THURSDAY
Moon Age Day 22 • Moon Sign Gemini

am ....

pm ....

You probably feel the need today to spend some time on social or pleasurable pursuits of your own invention and this can cause some resentment coming from the direction of your partner or close friends. This forms a tricky situation and you must decide early how you are going to split your time.

147

6 FRIDAY
Moon Age Day 23 ‹ Moon Sign Gemini

am ....

pm ....

The optimistic frame of mind you find yourself in is maintained today, particularly since heart-warming news, possibly from far away, will be coming to your doorstep now. This, together with other happenings puts you in a good mood for the remainder of the day. Social discussions help to stimulate your grey matter no end.

7 SATURDAY
Moon Age Day 24 ‹ Moon Sign Gemini

am ....

pm ....

Despite the arrival of the weekend, you have a hectic schedule to keep to, organising your time carefully and keeping appointments wherever possible. It would be all to easy to allow others and situations generally to side-track you from important priorities, especially with pleasantries which abound just at present.

8 SUNDAY
Moon Age Day 25 ‹ Moon Sign Cancer

am ....

pm ....

An easy going and carefree approach to daily life is what you can expect from yourself now; you can bring out the most appealing qualities in others while you are at it. It is easy to find compliments to pass on to others and there are important meetings and talks which go mostly in your favour.

← NEGATIVE TREND						POSITIVE TREND →				
-5	-4	-3	-2	-1		+1	+2	+3	+4	+5
					LOVE					
					MONEY					
					LUCK					
					VITALITY					

9 MONDAY
Moon Age Day 26 ‹ Moon Sign Cancer

am ....

pm ....

Things move on in your chart, and your Virgoan leadership qualities are called into play on and off for the days ahead. You may not consider yourself to be a natural leader, though others will have a different opinion of the situation and will be only too willing to rely on the comments that you make.

10 TUESDAY
Moon Age Day 27 ‹ Moon Sign Leo

am ....

pm ....

Make certain that you keep abreast of news and views concerning happenings in the vicinity of your work and home too. A good day for a chat, and for drawing far more out of what people are saying than their words alone would tend to imply. It is the intuitive Vrigo subject who really shows today.

11 WEDNESDAY
Moon Age Day 28 ‹ Moon Sign Leo

am ....

pm ....

The lunar high comes along again, bringing high spirits and much optimism. Self confidence is not lacking and you are able to pat yourself on the back as a result of successes from the recent past. A bright and sunny day from a social view-point and you have plenty of opportunity and energy to get things done in and around the home.

12 THURSDAY
Moon Age Day 29 ‹ Moon Sign Leo

am ....

pm ....

What you learn today can be turned to your advantage. Your objectives are sensible, and the goals that you aim for are modest. Because you are in such a positive frame of mind, you not only achieve what you intend, but probably much more besides. Friends are apt to do unexpected favours.

13 FRIDAY
Moon Age Day 0 ‹ Moon Sign Virgo

am ....

pm ....

The Moon still hangs on in there in your own sign of Virgo, and it has plenty to offer yet in terms of the potential successes that you have been noticing for the last couple of days. Around and about, you are happy to be out there in the mainstream of life, and doing what you can to cheer others up and keep them happy.

14 SATURDAY
Moon Age Day 1 ‹ Moon Sign Virgo

am ....

pm ....

Social meetings and even important family get-togethers thrive in an atmosphere of mutual understanding. Just about everyone who you meet is in a mood for compromise and will be able to concede points that they appear to have felt very strongly about in the past. Practical issues can be more demanding.

15 SUNDAY
Moon Age Day 2 ‹ Moon Sign Libra

am ....

pm ....

Unexpected points of disagreement are more or less inevitable today and particularly so in a personal relationship sense. Although you are quite willing to debate all situations, others are not so sensible or so logical at present. The one thing that you won't be willing to tolerate at the moment is any form of emotional blackmail.

← NEGATIVE TREND							POSITIVE TREND →			
-5	-4	-3	-2	-1		+1	+2	+3	+4	+5
					LOVE					
					MONEY					
					LUCK					
					VITALITY					

16 MONDAY   *Moon Age Day 3 ‹ Moon Sign Libra*

am ....

pm ....

Now that the trends turn even more in your favour, you are likely to be feeling more energetic than ever. A competitive side to your nature, so often under lock and key, is now starting to show itself more and more. In every practical sense, this should be a positive start to the working week.

17 TUESDAY   *Moon Age Day 4 ‹ Moon Sign Libra*

am ....

pm ....

The attitude of colleagues or associates can broaden your understanding of the world at large and you should treat today as a potentially valuable learning experience. Long journeys of any sort would be particularly favourable, either in reality, or still in the planning stage.

18 WEDNESDAY   *Moon Age Day 5 ‹ Moon Sign Scorpio*

am .... FREE FROM CAPTIVITY ....

pm ....

Even apparently casual conversations can now feed you with really good ideas. Stopping to have a chat to almost anyone you know could be useful, and you probably will not feel like giving yourself exclusively to the job in hand in any case. Socially, you should be enjoying an especially high profile.

19 THURSDAY   *Moon Age Day 6 ‹ Moon Sign Scorpio*

am ....

pm ....

In social settings you clearly have much to say for yourself, and even on those occasions where others do not agree with you, there should still be an attentive audience and plenty of cheers from the gallery. You really do not mind being in the social limelight at present and should not be over-anxious.

20 FRIDAY
Moon Age Day 7 ‹ Moon Sign Sagittarius

am ....

pm ....

A sneak preview of the days to come shows the weeks ahead to be
probably the best part of the year so far for you, and there is great
determination and energy now within the ranks of Virgo. A swifter
kind of progress now becomes possible, with plenty of help coming
from directions that are very important.

21 SATURDAY
Moon Age Day 8 ‹ Moon Sign Sagittarius

am ....

pm ....

Most Virgoans should be feeling good and looking at life in a very
positive way just now. The arrival of the weekend means plenty to
keep you occupied, and with some signs that personal freedom is now
on the increase, perhaps you might choose to spend some time out
and about.

22 SUNDAY
Moon Age Day 9 ‹ Moon Sign Capricorn

am ....

pm ....

All pleasurable activities and leisure pursuits are very favourably
highlighted today. This is after all a Sunday, and unless you are the
sort of Virgoan who has to work at the weekend, you would be
happiest leaving some responsibilities alone for a while in favour of
doing whatever takes your fancy.

← *NEGATIVE TREND*   *POSITIVE TREND* →

-5	-4	-3	-2	-1		+1	+2	+3	+4	+5
					LOVE					
					MONEY					
					LUCK					
					VITALITY					

23 MONDAY   *Moon Age Day 10 ‹ Moon Sign Capricorn*

am ....

pm ....

You start the new working week with positive trends, so you should be looking good and feeling fit. Partly because of the ambience you exhibit, you tend to get a good reception from almost everyone you meet. Don't be frightened to take advantage of your powers of persuasion and influence wherever you are.

24 TUESDAY   *Moon Age Day 11 ‹ Moon Sign Capricorn*

am ....

pm ....

Others seem to be pushing their weight around, particularly at work and in professional situations generally. It might be best to keep quiet and avoid conflicts which can get out of hand at present. In any case you would not want to be on the losing side of any argument. Domestic situations more than make up for difficulties.

25 WEDNESDAY   *Moon Age Day 12 ‹ Moon Sign Aquarius*

am ....

pm ....

Conflict between what partners expect of you and what you want of yourself, are more or less inevitable now. Wherever possible you should try to achieve a happy medium. There is a financial consideration - be careful who you lend money to. Planetary indictations are that you may not get it back for quite some time.

26 THURSDAY   *Moon Age Day 13 ‹ Moon Sign Aquarius*

am ....

pm ....

More give and take is now necessary, both in relationships and in associations of a more professional nature. For once you are certainly thinking too much about number one and others will not fail to remind you of your duties and obligations if this proves to be the case. This is a period when finances can fluctuate wildly.

27 FRIDAY

Moon Age Day 14 ‹ Moon Sign Pisces

am ....

pm ....

Most obligations to others are carried out gladly and with high spirits. In fact most tasks tend to be a labour of love at present because you are being active and industrious. Personal or even professional involvements are also positively highlighted and this is generally a day for getting things done in a flamboyant manner.

28 SATURDAY

Moon Age Day 15 ‹ Moon Sign Pisces

am ....

pm ....

There may be heavy, although not altogether unexpected, domestic and family demands made upon you this weekend. Though you see these as serious responsibilities, do bear in mind that an all work and no play attitude is not to be advised at present. Even if you have to delay decisions until later, you need time to be yourself.

29 SUNDAY

Moon Age Day 16 ‹ Moon Sign Aries

am ....

pm ....

There are all sorts of people about who want to make rash promises, or who appear to be in a position to do you favours. Self reliance is now the best way to accomplish your ideas, though in situations where you must be dependent on others, don't expect miracles. A confident attitude is important.

← NEGATIVE TREND						POSITIVE TREND →				
-5	-4	-3	-2	-1		+1	+2	+3	+4	+5
					LOVE					
					MONEY					
					LUCK					
					VITALITY					

30 MONDAY   *Moon Age Day 17 ‹ Moon Sign Aries*

am ....

pm ....

Your get-up-and-go attitude does much to help personal matters move smoothly and easily today. Don't be afraid to ask favours from influential people as you may be surprised at the positive responses you are getting. Your love life can turn out to be more exciting than you think and particularly so if you make a special effort.

1 TUESDAY   *Moon Age Day 18 ‹ Moon Sign Taurus*

am ....

pm ....

Family or domestic issues tend to be fairly troublesome and your partner may have thoughts on their mind which run contrary to your own opinions. Spending time away from work seems to be something that cheers you at present. Do try to discover what others are thinking and make time for important personal discussions.

2 WEDNESDAY   *Moon Age Day 19 ‹ Moon Sign Taurus*

am ....

pm ....

You have some ideas today that can be seen as being both clever and creative. This is particularly the case with regard to attracting more money and towards getting the material things you want from life. You tend to take on a 'nothing ventured, nothing gained' attitude and money matters show genuine and sustained improvement.

3 THURSDAY   *Moon Age Day 20 ‹ Moon Sign Gemini*

am ....

pm ....

Some disagreements can now arise regarding money and the present associations dogging your life at present means that both sides in such situations will be fairly unwilling to back down. Although you should stand your ground in any potential conflict, don't stubbornly refuse to budge just for the sake of your own pride.

4 FRIDAY
Moon Age Day 21 ‹ Moon Sign Gemini

am ....

pm ....

There is news coming in today that can turn out to be a real eyebrow
raiser. If this is regarding a mutual friend it will be best kept to
yourself. Secrets are not hard to hold at present, even if there are
certain individuals around who are trying to make you spill the
beans. Attend to a variety of interests now.

5 SATURDAY
Moon Age Day 22 ‹ Moon Sign Cancer

am ....

pm ....

It might be time to take a good look at your finances, particularly
since there are elements that you have overlooked. At the same
time, you are displaying some ingenious ideas to the world at large,
and if these involve attracting money to yourself, then put them into
action.

6 SUNDAY
Moon Age Day 23 ‹ Moon Sign Cancer

am ....

pm ....

Complicated issues arise at home with regard to all practical
matters. However, if you choose your words skilfully, this is a
situation that can easily be side-stepped. Out-witting others comes
almost as second nature now and you do need to be very subtle if
any potential conflict brings you face to face with someone you know
to be of a powerful nature.

← NEGATIVE TREND							POSITIVE TREND →			
-5	-4	-3	-2	-1		+1	+2	+3	+4	+5
					LOVE					
					MONEY					
					LUCK					
					VITALITY					

1996

YOUR MONTH AT A GLANCE

The twelve numbered boxes represent the important areas in your life. The key to the numbers you will find beneath the panel. A Sun above the number indicates that opportunities are around. A Cloud below the number, that you should be a bit defensive. Nothing above or below and life will be pretty ordinary.

		☀		☀							
1	2	3	4	5	6	7	8	9	10	11	12
				☁					☁		☁

KEY

1 Strength of Personality	7 One to One Relationships
2 Personal Finance	8 Questioning, Thinking & Deciding
3 Useful Information Gathering	9 External Influences / Education
4 Domestic Affairs	10 Career Aspirations
5 Pleasure & Romance	11 Teamwork Activities
6 Effective Work & Health	12 Unconscious Impulses

OCTOBER HIGHS AND LOWS

Here, I show how the rhythm of the Moon will affect you this month. Like the tide, your energies and abilities will rise and fall with its pattern. When it is above the date line, go-for-it. When it is below the line you should be resting.

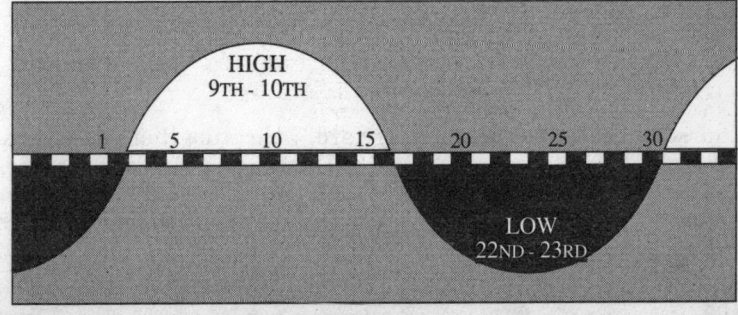

7 MONDAY

Moon Age Day 24 • Moon Sign Leo

am ....

pm ....

A loved one is inclined to feel rather insecure today and will need constant assurance from you if they are not be suffering quite a lot in one way or another. This sort of support is not at all difficult for you to offer when you are in the mood, and you have rarely been more supportive than you are at present.

8 TUESDAY

Moon Age Day 25 • Moon Sign Leo

am ....

pm ....

With a lighthearted and carefree attitude to everyday events, you should see this as an excellent time for leisure, possibly even for celebrations of one sort or another. You are well thought of socially, actively seeking and finding the limelight. Most important of all, you can establish a good balance between pleasure and business.

9 WEDNESDAY

Moon Age Day 26 • Moon Sign Virgo

am ....

pm ....

The Moon returns to your sign, so that energy and enthusiasm in abundance attend your life today. Put your best foot forward and press on with all current plans with the vigour that is so typical of your sign at the moment. Your ability to attract fortunate situations is certainly in operation right now.

10 THURSDAY

Moon Age Day 27 • Moon Sign Virgo

am ....

pm ....

Thursday shows you pushing forward, indicating that you offer an attractive face to the world at large. Unattached Virgoans should be finding new romantic proposals on offer, possibly associated in some way with work. For all of you the feeling of optimism runs high, though you are unable to go it alone.

11 FRIDAY

Moon Age Day 28 ‹ Moon Sign Virgo

am ....

pm ....

The emotional peak is followed by one relating to personal popularity. You might find yourself to be everyone's favourite person at present and though this could lead to some jealousy or envy coming from the direction of others, this is generally a time for harmony and enjoying good times.

12 SATURDAY

Moon Age Day 0 ‹ Moon Sign Libra

am ....

pm ....

Despite the arrival of Saturday, this is very much a business as usual sort of day. Working Taureans can make favourable progress, but even in this case you should not allow this to prevent you from considering new plans of a more social nature. Friends may rely upon you quite heavily and you should be happy to offer support.

13 SUNDAY

Moon Age Day 1 ‹ Moon Sign Libra

am ....

pm ....

Time spent alone, or perhaps with someone who is very dear to you is time well spent. Put serious obligations back in the cupboard when it proves possible to do so and don't be surprised if all practical matters appear to be a chore just now. Turning down social invitations is unavoidable, but will not cause problems if your motives are suspect.

← NEGATIVE TREND								POSITIVE TREND →			
-5	-4	-3	-2	-1			+1	+2	+3	+4	+5
					LOVE						
					MONEY						
					LUCK						
					VITALITY						

14 MONDAY

Moon Age Day 2 ‹ Moon Sign Scorpio

am ....

pm ....

Your mind is almost anywhere but on the task in hand, particularly regarding work plans or practical matters generally. It is easy to become bored with the hum-drum reality of life and the secret is to find something new and pleasant to distract you. Keep such considerations to the correct time of course and avoid being pushy.

15 TUESDAY

Moon Age Day 3‹ Moon Sign Scorpio

am ....

pm ....

You can now find yourself involved much more than usual in a colleague's or friend's emotional problems. The private lives of others become public as far as you are concerned and your assistance is being counted on. You can certainly impart some of your age-old wisdom today and it is well received.

16 WEDNESDAY

Moon Age Day 4‹ Moon Sign Sagittarius

am ....

pm ....

There may be unexpected emotional issued to contend with today. Romance throws up the odd problem, some of which prove to be self-created. Take the time and trouble necessary to sort them out carefully and also get your priorities right at work, where there is much at stake. Continued reliance on others is tedious now.

17 THURSDAY

Moon Age Day 5 ‹ Moon Sign Sagittarius

am ....

pm ....

Some caution is necessary as you are accused today of thinking about number one. It is possible that such an accusation comes from someone who is used to having all their own way with you, which is much less likely just at present. As long as you can justify your own actions to yourself, there is really no problem.

18 FRIDAY
Moon Age Day 6 ‹ Moon Sign Capricorn

am ....

pm ....

Meetings and appointments may need double checking. With a tendency to overlook necessary details, talks or more casual discussions stimulate your emotions, leading ultimately to strong words on both sides. Where others are concerned, you are inclined to act as a go-between and may just get yourself in social hot water as a result.

19 SATURDAY
Moon Age Day 7 ‹ Moon Sign Capricorn

am ....

pm ....

All social discussions, or important negotiations go smoothly as you are so much in touch with the thoughts and feelings of those close to you. Even usually awkward colleagues can be turned to your advantage with care, and your intuitions will tell you all you need to know about the world around you. Any lack of trust is temporary.

20 SUNDAY
Moon Age Day 8 ‹ Moon Sign Aquarius

am ....

pm ....

Some rather tense aspects cropping up in your solar chart indicate that others are almost certain to point to what they see as flaws within your nature. Since this aspect can also make you more sensitive than might normally be the case, it would be a good idea not to take too much notice of what is being said.

← *NEGATIVE TREND*   *POSITIVE TREND* →

-5	-4	-3	-2	-1			+1	+2	+3	+4	+5
					LOVE						
					MONEY						
					LUCK						
					VITALITY						

21 MONDAY

Moon Age Day 9 ‹ Moon Sign Aquarius

am ....

pm ....

People who are important to you, if only in a professional sense, have something important to put upon your shoulders. You will really not want to let anyone down just at present and can work minor miracles if you choose to set your mind to it. Long-term changes could be looked at realistically in the next day or two.

22 TUESDAY

Moon Age Day 10 ‹ Moon Sign Aquarius

am ....

pm ....

The lunar low arrives along with Tuesday, making it necessary to put present schemes on the shelf for the next couple of days. This is an ideal period to be finishing off routine tasks left over from the past and look to your partner to come through where your own efforts seem to get you nowhere.

23 WEDNESDAY

Moon Age Day 11 ‹ Moon Sign Pisces

am ....

pm ....

With the lunar low still around, you are not at your most physically energetic to meet the working week. Routine tasks will be the best ones to undertake now, leaving important decision making until later. Setbacks to routines can be aggravating, though not in the long term. Count on the support of others for a while.

24 THURSDAY

Moon Age Day 12 ‹ Moon Sign Pisces

am ....

pm ....

Divided loyalties now become possible, especially if you allow yourself to get between loved ones and friends when any sort of dispute is likely. Perhaps it would be best to avoid any such situation and to do your best to pour oil on troubled waters if you cannot help being drawn into the situation somehow.

25 FRIDAY
Moon Age Day 13 ‹ Moon Sign Aries

am ....

pm ....

The most casual social conversations can become heated now, as combined influences at present in your chart, create a more combative Virgoan than would generally be the case. Nevertheless you don't have all the answers and must allow for necessary differences of opinion.

26 SATURDAY
Moon Age Day 14 ‹ Moon Sign Aries

am ....

pm ....

Although the weekend is here, don't be surprised if some professional issues get the go-ahead now. In most areas of your life, you are now in a position to affect the course of events. Your personal intuition is high and others are inclined to turn to you for leadership. Those in authority should be impressed.

27 SUNDAY
Moon Age Day 15 ‹ Moon Sign Taurus

am ....

pm ....

Hunches tend to be worth listening to, and can be acted upon in all cases. There is a side to your mind that other types do not enjoy to the same extent, so you really cannot expect others to rely quite so much on gut reactions as you tend to do. Certain aspects of the past must be faced up to at the present time.

← NEGATIVE TREND						POSITIVE TREND →				
-5	-4	-3	-2	-1		+1	+2	+3	+4	+5
					LOVE					
					MONEY					
					LUCK					
					VITALITY					

28 MONDAY
Moon Age Day 16 ‹ Moon Sign Taurus

am ....

pm ....

At the start of a new and favourable working week, you can almost instantly make a good impression on colleagues or associates. Good news arrives regarding ambitions and plans of a professional nature. It should also be an advantageous time financially with money resources boosted by an agreeable and compromising atmosphere.

29 TUESDAY
Moon Age Day 17 ‹ Moon Sign Gemini

am ....

pm ....

The best time of all to put new ideas into action, no matter if they are large or small. A colleague or a friend can be relied upon to take your side and help you out in any way that they can. You can also reap some of the benefits from the help and support that you have been so willing to show to others this month.

30 WEDNESDAY
Moon Age Day 18 ‹ Moon Sign Gemini

am ....

pm ....

Not all the help that you require today comes from the directions that you would expect, and so you should get yourself used to the prospects of some surprises before the day is out. A good time to be re-establishing social contacts that have fallen by the wayside recently, and for making new friends at some stage.

31 THURSDAY
Moon Age Day 19 ‹ Moon Sign Cancer

am ....

pm ....

At the end of October you need to toe the line as circumstances conspire to limit your freedom. Avoid planning too far ahead and ensure that your obligations and duties regarding others are attended to before you move on. Taking on too many commitments now would certainly be a mistake and a little rest would be of good.

1 FRIDAY
Moon Age Day 20 ‹ Moon Sign Cancer

am ....

pm ....

Perhaps you are not quite so sensible at the start of this month as you were earlier, mainly because you do not care for the attitude of those around you. This could be sort of Friday when many Virgoans would be seeking a little solitude, and there is no doubt that you can make gains from being alone.

2 SATURDAY
Moon Age Day 21 ‹ Moon Sign Cancer

am ....

pm ....

A few problems are turned round cleverly now meaning that rewards come especially from the direction of your house and home during the next week or two. Some slight tendency to be impulsive should be more than countered by an ability to get things done in a constructive manner, both at home and at work.

3 SUNDAY
Moon Age Day 22 ‹ Moon Sign Leo

am ....

pm ....

You now have the chance to get yourself out of some sort of financial rut and would be well advised to do so. In amongst thoughts about the money aspects of your life you should not lose sight of the personal side of life. In many respects this has rarely been better, though there could be niggles at home.

← NEGATIVE TREND						POSITIVE TREND →				
-5	-4	-3	-2	-1		+1	+2	+3	+4	+5
					LOVE					
					MONEY					
					LUCK					
					VITALITY					

1996

YOUR MONTH AT A GLANCE

The twelve numbered boxes represent the important areas in your life. The key to the numbers you will find beneath the panel. A Sun above the number indicates that opportunities are around. A Cloud below the number, that you should be a bit defensive. Nothing above or below and life will be pretty ordinary.

		☀		☀		☀					
1	2	3	4	5	6	7	8	9	10	11	12
					☁				☁		

KEY

1 Strength of Personality
2 Personal Finance
3 Useful Information Gathering
4 Domestic Affairs
5 Pleasure & Romance
6 Effective Work & Health

7 One to One Relationships
8 Questioning, Thinking & Deciding
9 External Influences / Education
10 Career Aspirations
11 Teamwork Activities
12 Unconscious Impulses

NOVEMBER HIGHS AND LOWS

Here, I show how the rhythm of the Moon will affect you this month. Like the tide, your energies and abilities will rise and fall with its pattern. When it is above the date line, go-for-it. When it is below the line you should be resting.

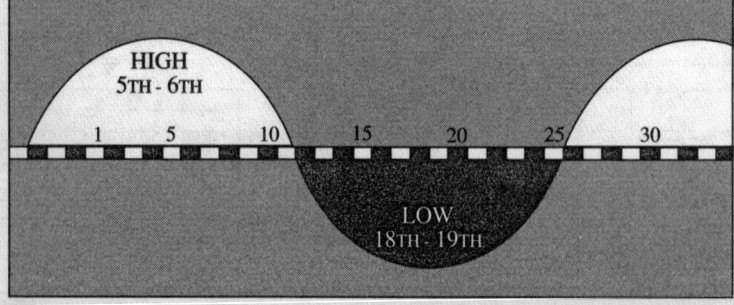

4 MONDAY

Moon Age Day 23 • Moon Sign Leo

am ....

pm ....

Minor financial gains are possible, and as your mind is working very quickly at present, you should be in a good position to make the best of them. Loved-ones may be more than willing to let you know how much they care about you and of course you will want to show them much affection in return.

5 TUESDAY

Moon Age Day 24 • Moon Sign Virgo

am ....

pm ....

An excellent day to get stuck into all those jobs that have been hanging around for so long. With the lunar high now working for you positively, you will also want to make the most of new opportunities that come your way. There is more than a chance that you will find finances strengthening significantly.

6 WEDNESDAY

Moon Age Day 25 • Moon Sign Virgo

am ....

pm ....

Good luck appears to be easier to find, as the week reaches its half way stage. Almost everyone that you come across seems to be in the right mood to do you some favours, and you can take advantage of the fact, without feeling that you are putting on the people concerned.

7 THURSDAY

Moon Age Day 26 • Moon Sign Virgo

am ....

pm ....

Trying to please everyone at once could again prove to be something of a problem for you today. The people with whom you live and work could be expecting far more of you in some ways than you are either willing or able to give. Important personal plans should be pressed ahead with, no matter what.

8 FRIDAY
Moon Age Day 27 ‹ Moon Sign Libra

am ....

pm ....

What a good day this would be for spring-cleaning, even though the Autumn is now well and truly here. You may find that it is the way you think that needs a little organising, but there are people around who can be of significant assistance. A really difficult person may cease to have a place in your life quite soon.

9 SATURDAY
Moon Age Day 28 ‹ Moon Sign Libra

am ....

pm ....

You can work long and hard this weekend in pursuit of your own idea of success. There are few people about who would have sufficient strength of character to tell you that you are not doing the things that you should be, though if you are perceptive, you could hardly fail to notice their attitudes.

10 SUNDAY
Moon Age Day 29 ‹ Moon Sign Scorpio

am ....

pm ....

People want to set themselves up to prove that they can do certain things better than you can. In most respects there is no competition and you will have nothing to prove. However you can be very determined on occasions and could easily rise to the bait in some way before the day is finally over.

← NEGATIVE TREND						POSITIVE TREND →				
-5	-4	-3	-2	-1		+1	+2	+3	+4	+5
					LOVE					
					MONEY					
					LUCK					
					VITALITY					

11 MONDAY   *Moon Age Day 0 ‹ Moon Sign Scorpio*

am ....

pm ....

A high profile day is probably on offer for most Virgo subjects now, and your ability to get on well with others is especially worthy of note. Even so, it is important not to agree with others simply for the sake of doing so. Your own opinion proves to be important to most people in any case.

12 TUESDAY   *Moon Age Day 1 ‹ Moon Sign Sagittarius*

am ....

pm ....

Life speeds up. Communication becomes easier with present trends predominating. So much so, that colleagues and friends alike will have great difficulty in keeping you quiet. A jokey atmosphere prevails, perpetuated by your present attitude and the involvement of new and interesting people who come on the scene.

13 WEDNESDAY   *Moon Age Day 2 ‹ Moon Sign Sagittarius*

am ....

pm ....

Others could appear to be moving forward at your expense. However, look around you because later on your partner, or close friends, can prove to be most helpful. Some residual frustration now merely serves as an incentive for future efforts on your part and patience is required today.

14 THURSDAY   *Moon Age Day 3 ‹ Moon Sign Sagittarius*

am ....

pm ....

Anxious for new experiences, for fresh fields and pastures new; anything old, unusual or curious captivates your imagination now. Your powers of intuition are at a peak and life's natural magic is all around. Use this period wisely because it is not the sort of time that crops up all that often.

15 FRIDAY

Moon Age Day 4 ‹ Moon Sign Capricorn

am ....

pm ....

There are generous offers about, many of them pointing in your direction. Financial propositions deserve a second look, though all situations need to be checked carefully before final decisions are made. This is a productive time, when you are likely to have your hands full, both domestically and with regard to the family.

16 SATURDAY

Moon Age Day 5 ‹ Moon Sign Capricorn

am ....

pm ....

Despite significant confidence and strength of character, when dealing with everyday situations, the competitive quality of your nature tends to be overplayed. Today you can see challenges where there are none, and would be well advised to find positive outlets for excess energy. Important friends have some good ideas.

17 SUNDAY

Moon Age Day 6 ‹ Moon Sign Aquarius

am ....

pm ....

Take extra care when discussing delicate personal issues, relating to close family members. The more straight forward you are in your approach, though without being blunt, the better. Joint financial plans could be somewhat unsettling and corrective action is required if you are not to create a situation that could be worrying later.

← NEGATIVE TREND						POSITIVE TREND →				
-5	-4	-3	-2	-1		+1	+2	+3	+4	+5
					LOVE					
					MONEY					
					LUCK					
					VITALITY					

18 MONDAY *Moon Age Day 7 ‹ Moon Sign Aquarius*

am ....

pm ....
At the start of a new working week, it isn't exactly easy to find that
the lunar low is causing some lethargy. Hold back with major plans
until you recognise that the time is right, because you can achieve
much more at the beginning of this week by simply sitting and
watching the world go by, and then by acting later.

19 TUESDAY *Moon Age Day 8 ‹ Moon Sign Pisces*

am ....

pm ....
Minor hold-ups are still likely, though this does not mean that you
should kiss goodbye to any form of progress today. On the contrary,
it is below the surface of ordinary life that you can expect to see
some real progress being made, and also through relationships,
which should be working out well. A time to plan.

20 WEDNESDAY *Moon Age Day 9 ‹ Moon Sign Pisces*

am ....

pm ....
Your life partner, or a close friend, can easily bring out the best in
you today. Others seem determined to make social plans on your
account and for once you are happy to let them have their own way.
Life shows a distinct lack of pressure. Take the lead in social
arrangements requiring your special touch.

21 THURSDAY *Moon Age Day 10 ‹ Moon Sign Aries*

am ....

pm ....
All practical projects will now show a swifter progress than of late.
Today's decisions spring from an accurate assessment of situations
and lead to more definite actions in the fullness of time. Where
setbacks do occur, you should realise that these merely modify your
opinions and strengthen your will.

22 FRIDAY
Moon Age Day 11 ‹ Moon Sign Aries

am ....

pm ....

You do need to pay more attention to detail and to keep you hand on the pulse of all of life's activities. This means splitting your time rather carefully and not being willing to rest on your laurels, even regarding situations that are turning out well. There should be time to socialise and to be the centre of attraction later in the day.

23 SATURDAY
Moon Age Day 12 ‹ Moon Sign Taurus

am ....

pm ....

This should be a very good day for shopping for the home, or for any sort of DIY project, but you can't expect everyone to agree with your point of view at present. Some selfish attitude are likely at this time, but you could avoid major upsets of disagreements further down the line. Certain people rely upon you heavily.

24 SUNDAY
Moon Age Day 13 ‹ Moon Sign Taurus

am ....

pm ....

A physical boost comes along, during which you should feel energetic and ready for almost anything. Competitiveness is almost certain with trends being what they are, but don't allow this to get out of hand, particularly in social situations. There are points to be proved today, but there is also the tendency to overstep the mark.

← *NEGATIVE TREND*　　　　　*POSITIVE TREND* →

-5	-4	-3	-2	-1			+1	+2	+3	+4	+5
					LOVE						
					MONEY						
					LUCK						
					VITALITY						

25 MONDAY　　　　*Moon Age Day 14 ‹ Moon Sign Gemini*

am ....

pm ....

All team work and co-operative ventures bring out the best in you at the moment. You will also find that you need to express your caring and sharing side. A close friend could have some inspiring news to impart which puts you in a favourable frame of mind. In professional matters it's business as usual.

26 TUESDAY　　　　*Moon Age Day 15 ‹ Moon Sign Gemini*

am ....

pm ....

Your own work, plus the obligations you feel towards other people can be something of chore, though the rewards come further down the line as a result of both past and present efforts. Consideration of the plans put forward by colleagues may have to wait until you have more time to think.

27 WEDNESDAY　　　　*Moon Age Day 16 ‹ Moon Sign Gemini*

am ....

pm ....

Don't let today's actions be dictated by emotional impulses on any level, which is one of the reasons why family discussions may not work out too well now. The other important thing to remember at the moment is that you can't please everyone all of the time and so it may be rather futile to even try. Give and take is important.

28 THURSDAY　　　　*Moon Age Day 17 ‹ Moon Sign Cancer*

am ....

pm ....

Much of the goodwill that you have shown to others in the past now comes back to you tenfold. Despite your popularity you may be somewhat more ambitious than is really good for you. A hard-headed approach is not advisable at present and harsh words would be out of place. Some small disputes can prove to be tedious but are necessary.

29 FRIDAY
Moon Age Day 18 ‹ Moon Sign Cancer

am ....

pm ....

Do your very best to get away from routines wherever possible, even though you want to maintain a business like approach to life. What is most important is the opportunity to enjoy yourself at some stage, probably mixing business and pleasure in ways that benefit others as well as yourself.

30 SATURDAY
Moon Age Day 19 ‹ Moon Sign Leo

am ....

pm ....

Self sacrificing or charitable gestures seem to be the order of the day and are presented with no strings attached. It is possible that others could misconstrue your actions and so it is very important to explain yourself. This should not be necessary in the case of close friends or relatives who are more likely to rely on your judgement.

1 SUNDAY
Moon Age Day 20 ‹ Moon Sign Leo

am ....

pm ....

You could be a little over emotional, so ensure reactions are not out of proportion to any given situation. Look in the direction of your partner or a close relative who is able to provide tender loving care and will be happy to do so in return for similar favours shown by you.

1996

YOUR MONTH AT A GLANCE

The twelve numbered boxes represent the important areas in your life. The key to the numbers you will find beneath the panel. A Sun above the number indicates that opportunities are around. A Cloud below the number, that you should be a bit defensive. Nothing above or below and life will be pretty ordinary.

1	2	3	4	5	6	7	8	9	10	11	12

(Suns above boxes 3, 5, 7; Clouds below boxes 2, 8)

KEY

1 Strength of Personality
2 Personal Finance
3 Useful Information Gathering
4 Domestic Affairs
5 Pleasure & Romance
6 Effective Work & Health
7 One to One Relationships
8 Questioning, Thinking & Deciding
9 External Influences / Education
10 Career Aspirations
11 Teamwork Activities
12 Unconscious Impulses

DECEMBER HIGHS AND LOWS

Here, I show how the rhythm of the Moon will affect you this month. Like the tide, your energies and abilities will rise and fall with its pattern. When it is above the date line, go-for-it. When it is below the line you should be resting.

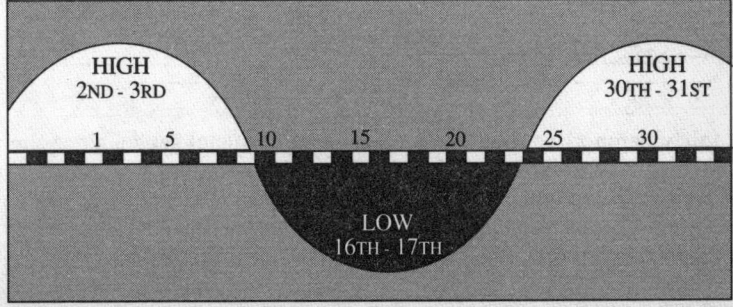

HIGH
2ND - 3RD

HIGH
30TH - 31ST

LOW
16TH - 17TH

2 MONDAY

Moon Age Day 21 • Moon Sign Leo

am ....

pm ....

A winning streak comes into your life courtesy of the lunar high and no matter what situation you find yourself faced with you should be equal to the task. Any changes to the basic structure of your life can be put into operation now. The relationships that you form prove to be comfortable.

3 TUESDAY

Moon Age Day 32 • Moon Sign Virgo

am ....

pm ....

Optimism remains high as the Moon remains for today in your sign. Good things should be coming your way now and there is a possible boost to your finances, which may not even be related to the effort you are willing to put in personally. Confidence should be much higher than you might expect.

4 WEDNESDAY

Moon Age Day 23 • Moon Sign Virgo

am ....

pm ....

Intimate relationships take on an especially warm and sincere feel today, which could be part of the reason that you are not taking the practical aspects of life quite as seriously as you will do in a day or two. Thoughts of Christmas captivate you, even so early in the month, and forward planning is necessary.

5 THURSDAY

Moon Age Day 24 • Moon Sign Libra

am ....

pm ....

A fairly demanding day, particularly in a financial sense, since there are certain decisions that you will have to make now that cannot be shared with anyone else. This does not mean that you find yourself isolated in a personal sense however, because there is plenty of companyavailable if you look for it.

6 FRIDAY
Moon Age Day 25 ‹ Moon Sign Libra

am ....

pm ....

There is little doubt that present trends in your solar chart have an enlivening effect on all romantic relationships and though the competitive edge remains in a professional sense, much of your day is spent in high spirits and good humour. A slower and slightly more methodical approach works well.

7 SATURDAY
Moon Age Day 26 ‹ Moon Sign Libra

am ....

pm ....

You now tend to be less in demand than has been the case for the last few days, probably not a bad situation considering that you need time to sit and think. Personal projects feature prominently in your thinking now and though finances ought to be relatively stable, this might not be a bad period for forward planning.

8 SUNDAY
Moon Age Day 27 ‹ Moon Sign Scorpio

am ....

pm ....

Unexpected demands come from the direction of loved ones, perhaps because on a Sunday you are taking more time out to look in this direction. The pace of events begins to speed up, even though the weekend does mean a little more time to do what takes your fancy. Don't be too ready to change your views.

← NEGATIVE TREND							POSITIVE TREND →			
-5	-4	-3	-2	-1		+1	+2	+3	+4	+5
					LOVE					
					MONEY					
					LUCK					
					VITALITY					

9 MONDAY
Moon Age Day 28 ‹ Moon Sign Scorpio

am ....

pm ....

Ever more entertaining company comes your way and you can look forward to a happy time to come, mostly because of the company that surrounds you at the time. Keep a watch out for invitations from both friends and acquaintances, but whilst you are looking ahead ensure that you do not over-commit yourself.

10 TUESDAY
Moon Age Day 0 ‹ Moon Sign Sagittarius

am ....

pm ....

For one reason or another, you may be trying to talk other people into doing things your way and this can prove to be a difficult situation. You may be forced into the position of taking a back seat and of assuming a low profile when it comes to decision making. For now at least, this would not be a bad thing.

11 WEDNESDAY
Moon Age Day 1 ‹ Moon Sign Sagittarius

am ....

pm ....

This is a day for encountering people who are able to contribute to your own feeling of professional success. Present planetary positions increase your communication skills and add to the chance of positive encounters and new friendships. Don't be reluctant to use any situation to your own advantage whenever you can.

12 THURSDAY
Moon Age Day 2 ‹ Moon Sign Capricorn

am ....

pm ....

You show a desire to be friendly to almost anyone you meet and yet much of what you have to say could come across as insincere. Nevertheless, even casual conversations can reveal some surprising and interesting information so it is worth keeping on talking. The hidden aspects of life are important.

13 FRIDAY　　　　　*Moon Age Day 3 ‹ Moon Sign Capricorn*

am ....

pm ....

Moving away from the rat-race, you are now quite anxious and able to let your hair down. In social gatherings you are the star attraction and the magnetic powers of your Mercurial personality are in evidence. Not a good day for attending to details but ideal for taking an over-view of your life.

14 SATURDAY　　　　*Moon Age Day 4 ‹ Moon Sign Aquarius*

am ....

pm ....

The power of your personal influence is strong, though leisure activities may not be quite as exciting as you had expected. Slight quirks in your nature now present show that you are keeping your deeper feelings under lock and key, which could prove to be a mistake if others think you are being deliberately secretive.

15 SUNDAY　　　　　*Moon Age Day 5 ‹ Moon Sign Aquarius*

am ....

pm ....

Swifter professional progress now becomes possible, even if this is not the case on a more personal level. Relatives come to have a greater need of the unique advice you are qualified to offer, whilst the attitudes of friends takes some thinking about. Social issues start to become very much more exciting.

← *NEGATIVE TREND*　　　　　*POSITIVE TREND* →

-5	-4	-3	-2	-1			+1	+2	+3	+4	+5
					LOVE						
					MONEY						
					LUCK						
					VITALITY						

16 MONDAY
Moon Age Day 6 ‹ Moon Sign Pisces

am ....

pm ....

Information received in a professional sense makes the path ahead
of you seem much more clear than it has been for a while. This
should be a good start to a positive and fairly busy working week,
though it does demand that you take things steadily for a day or so
at least. Plans for Christmas abound.

17 TUESDAY
Moon Age Day 7 ‹ Moon Sign Pisces

am ....

pm ....

A day for putting an end to efforts that have been under construction
in your life for some time. From now on you should have more time
to become involved in the schemes that others are putting forward,
and certainly there would appear to be individuals who are counting
on your assistance.

18 WEDNESDAY
Moon Age Day 8 ‹ Moon Sign Aries

am ....

pm ....

Partly as a result of the proximity of Christmas, the most agreeable
and compromising element of your nature is on display. You are
also quite chatty and excel in discussions of any sort. This is a
useful time to be playing go-between where warring parties in the
family, or amongst your friendship circle are concerned.

19 THURSDAY
Moon Age Day 9 ‹ Moon Sign Aries

am ....

pm ....

Business and pleasure come together to create one cohesive whole
just in advance of the festivities. Trying to look at only one aspect of
life could be rather counter-productive at present and the best plan
of all would be to go with the flow. Others need to share the
limelight, but will you let them?

20 FRIDAY
Moon Age Day 10 ‹ Moon Sign Tauus

am ....

pm ....

Good trends attend your life, courtesy of positive alterations in your attitude. In all career or practical matters, help should be forthcoming in furthering your aims and ambitions for the future. If ill-health has been a problem the situation should improve soon, allowing a more energetic approach.

21 SATURDAY
Moon Age Day 11 ‹ Moon Sign Taurus

am ....

pm ....

At the present time you are somewhat susceptible to negative emotional influences, and need to avoid taking your own moods too seriously. Striking the balance between optimism and pessimism is not easy at present and may not be assisted by the negative attitude of those around you. Stay realistic in your approach.

22 SUNDAY
Moon Age Day 12 ‹ Moon Sign Taurus

am ....

pm ....

Sunday is productive enough to keep you happy. Many of your efforts are going towards improving the quality of your life, so it isn't really necessary to be busy every moment of the day. Some good luck should be noticeable, especially in a financial sense, though gambling may not be a good idea for the present.

← NEGATIVE TREND　　　　*POSITIVE TREND →*

-5	-4	-3	-2	-1		+1	+2	+3	+4	+5
					LOVE					
					MONEY					
					LUCK					
					VITALITY					

23 MONDAY
Moon Age Day 13 ‹ Moon Sign Gemini

am ....

pm ....

Keeping your eye on the ball is difficult and it would be fair if people
accuse you of spreading yourself too thinly at present. Your work,
social life and personal involvements all demand attention, but you
will certainly have to put some issues on the shelf for a while and
concentrate on real priorities.

24 TUESDAY
Moon Age Day 14 ‹ Moon Sign Gemini

am ....

pm ....

There is an element of competition about today, and this is
especially true in the lives of working Virgoans. For all children of
Mercury, it is more likely that you will be persuading people at
home to follow your ideas, though by the evening it is enjoyment
that takes over.

25 WEDNESDAY
Moon Age Day 15 ‹ Moon Sign Cancer

am ....

pm ....

You enjoy Christmas Day best this time round if you are surrounded
by a whole host of people. This is not a good time to be on your own
too much, or to dwell on matters that have no real part to play in the
day. Coming to terms with the ideas of others is not difficult and
you accommodate most individuals.

26 THURSDAY
Moon Age Day 16 ‹ Moon Sign Cancer

am ....

pm ....

There could be a powerful psychic link with several people in your
vicinity and this allows you to know instinctively how they are
feeling. Acting according to your intuition would certainly be the
best course of action at present. Boxing Day brings mixed surprises,
and the chance to institute some changes.

27 FRIDAY

Moon Age Day 17 ‹ Moon Sign Cancer

am ....

pm ....

Now that some of the excitement has died down, it is possible to come to grips with practical and everyday matters, even though some reorganisation may be necessary in or around your home. In other respects this is a fulfilling day, and one that also allows some time to look ahead.

28 SATURDAY

Moon Age Day 18 ‹ Moon Sign Leo

am ....

pm ....

Able to keep in the midst of good company, you can also be on the receiving end of good news regarding family members and friends alike. Pleasant surprises abound and despite being very busy at home, short journeys and impromptu meetings can also bring benefits. Have a close look at some of your presents.

29 SUNDAY

Moon Age Day 19 ‹ Moon Sign Leo

am ....

pm ....

A fairly harmonious phase develops, especially in your love life. Sympathetic gestures are apparent in the direction of relatives, and close friends have ways and means of showing you how important you are to them. Don't dismiss your intuition out of hand because it is beginning to work very strongly.

← *NEGATIVE TREND*　　　　　　　　*POSITIVE TREND* →

-5	-4	-3	-2	-1		+1	+2	+3	+4	+5
					LOVE					
					MONEY					
					LUCK					
					VITALITY					

30 MONDAY

Moon Age Day 20 ‹ Moon Sign Virgo

am ....

pm ....

The most rewarding moments today come as a result of the closeness
you feel for those people who are most important in your life. It
might be a good idea to take a close look at your personal budget and
to make some provision for the extra expense that seems to
surround you just for the moment.

31 TUESDAY

Moon Age Day 21 ‹ Moon Sign Virgo

am ....

pm ....

Although you show a tendency now to place emphasis on short term
plans for the future, it might be useful to look at the year ahead as a
whole. Clear up unfinished business before the end of today and
then look forward to the excellent time that is promised, as long as
you put the effort in.

← NEGATIVE TREND							POSITIVE TREND →				
-5	-4	-3	-2	-1			+1	+2	+3	+4	+5
					LOVE						
					MONEY						
					LUCK						
					VITALITY						

RISING SIGNS
for VIRGO

Look along the top to find your date of birth, and down the side for hour (or two) if appropriate for Summer Time.

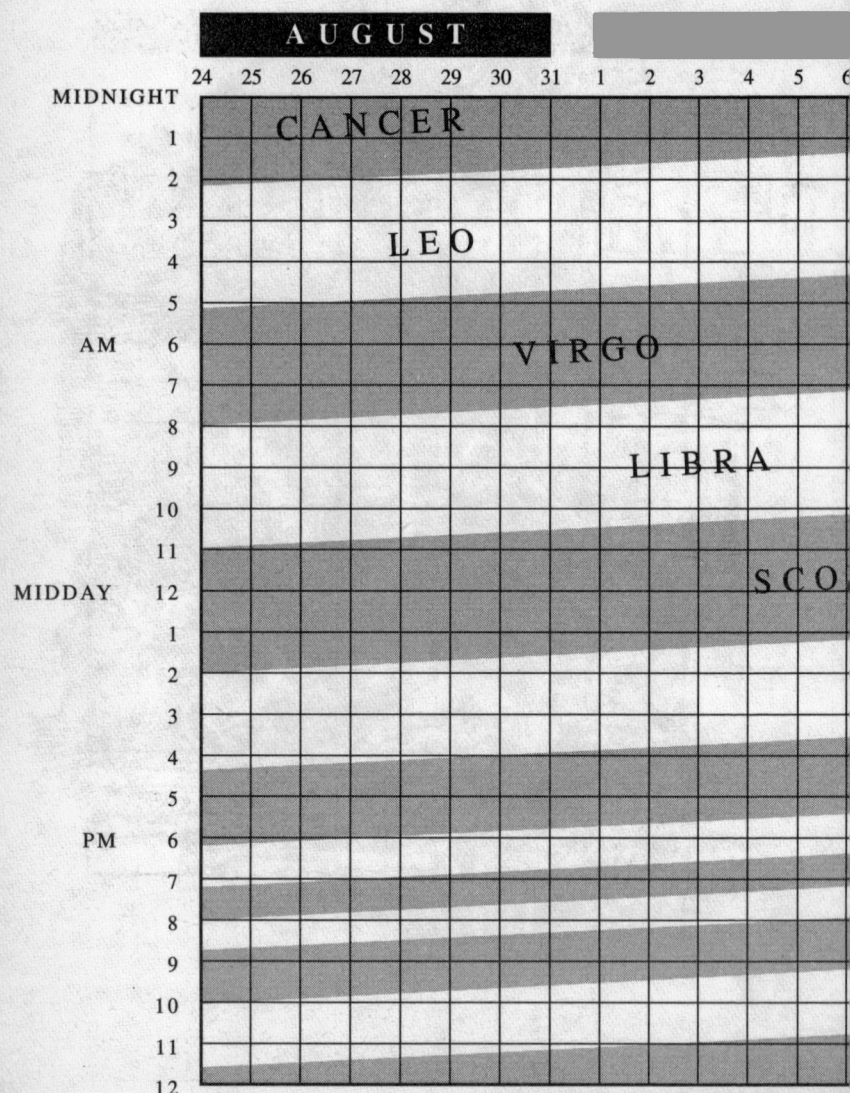

	AUGUST											
	24	25	26	27	28	29	30	31	1	2	3	4	5	6

MIDNIGHT

CANCER

LEO

AM 6

VIRGO

LIBRA

MIDDAY 12

SCO

PM 6

IT birth time. Where they cross is your Rising Sign. Don't forget to subtract an

| 8 | 9 | 10 | 11 | 12 | 13 | 14 | 15 | 16 | 17 | 18 | 19 | 20 | 21 | 22 | 23 |

0
1
2
3
4
5
6
7
8
9
10
11

O

12
1
2

GITTARIUS

3
4

CAPRICORN

5

AQUARIUS

6

PISCES

7

ARIES

TAURUS

8
9

GEMINI

10
11

CANCER

12

THE ZODIAC AT A GLANCE

Placed	Sign	Symbol	Glyph	Polarity	Element	Quality	Planet	Glyph	Metal	Stone	Opposite
1	Aries	Ram	♈	+	Fire	Cardinal	Mars	♂	Iron	Bloodstone	Libra
2	Taurus	Bull	♉	–	Earth	Fixed	Venus	♀	Copper	Sapphire	Scorpio
3	Gemini	Twins	♊	+	Air	Mutable	Mercury	☿	Mercury	Tiger's Eye	Sagittarius
4	Cancer	Crab	♋	–	Water	Cardinal	Moon	☽	Silver	Pearl	Capricorn
5	Leo	Lion	♌	+	Fire	Fixed	Sun	☉	Gold	Ruby	Aquarius
6	Virgo	Maiden	♍	–	Earth	Mutable	Mercury	☿	Mercury	Sardonyx	Pisces
7	Libra	Scales	♎	+	Air	Cardinal	Venus	♀	Copper	Sapphire	Aries
8	Scorpio	Scorpion	♏	–	Water	Fixed	Pluto	♇	Plutonium	Jasper	Taurus
9	Sagittarius	Archer	♐	+	Fire	Mutable	Jupiter	♃	Tin	Topaz	Gemini
10	Capricorn	Goat	♑	–	Earth	Cardinal	Saturn	♄	Lead	Black Onyx	Cancer
11	Aquarius	Waterbearer	♒	+	Air	Fixed	Uranus	♅	Uranium	Amethyst	Leo
12	Pisces	Fishes	♓	–	Water	Mutable	Neptune	♆	Tin	Moonstone	Virgo

THE ZODIAC, PLANETS AND CORRESPONDENCES

In the first column of the table of correspondence, I list the signs of the Zodiac as they order themselves around their circle; starting with Aries and finishing with Pisces. In the last column, I list the signs as they will appear as opposites to those in the first column. For example, the sign which will be positioned opposite Aries, in a circular chart will be Libra.

Each sign of the Zodiac is either positive or negative. This by no means suggests that they are either 'good' or 'bad', but that they are either extrovert, outgoing, masculine signs (positive), or introspective, receptive, feminine signs (negative).

Each sign of the Zodiac will belong to one of the four Elements: Fire, Air, Earth or Water. Fire signs are creative and enthusiastic; Air signs are mentally active and thoughtful; Earth signs are constructive and practical; Water signs are emotional and have strong feelings.

Each sign of the Zodiac also belongs to one of the Qualities: Cardinal, Fixed or Mutable. Cardinal signs are initiators and pioneers; Fixed signs are consistent and inflexible; Mutable signs are educators and live to serve.

So, each sign will be either positive or negative, and will belong to one of the Elements and to one of the Qualities. You can see from the table, for example, that Aries is a positive, Cardinal, Fire sign.

The table also shows which planets rule each sign. For example, Mars is the ruling planet of Aries. Each planet represents a particular facet of personality - Mars represents physical energy and drive - and the sign which it rules is the one with which it has most in common,

The table also shows which metals and gem stones are associated with, or correspond with the signs of the Zodiac. Again, the correspondence is made when a metal or stone possesses properties that are held in common with a particular sign of the Zodiac. This system of correspondences can be extended to encompass any group, whether animal, vegetable or mineral - as well as people! For example, each sign of the Zodiac is associated with particular flowers and herbs, with particular animals, with particular towns and countries, and so on.

It is an interesting exercise when learning about astrology, to guess which sign of the Zodiac rules a particular thing, by trying to match its qualities with the appropriate sign.

The News of the Future

1697 — *The Original Edition* — **1996**

PUBLISHED UNDER THE ORIGINAL COPYRIGHT DATING BACK TO 1697

1996 PREDICTIONS
HOME · WORLDWIDE · SPORTING

Foulsham's Original

OLD MOORE'S ALMANACK 1996

FOR THE YEAR — FOR THE YEAR

DR FRANCIS MOORE'S ALMANACK

Prophetic Hieroglyphic Engravings

WEATHER GUIDE—SUN & MOON TABLES—FAIRS
FLAT & CHASE RACE WINNERS
YOUR BIRTHDAY FORTUNE IN 1996
POOLS FORECAST

1996 — 1996

THE ANNUAL READERSHIP EXCEEDS THREE MILLION

BEWARE OF IMITATIONS OF THIS ORIGINAL ALMANACK

PUBLISHED BY
FOULSHAM, BENNETTS CLOSE, CIPPENHAM, SL1 5AP, BERKS.
OR TRADE SUPPLIES AT ALL WHOLESALE NEWSAGENTS.

In the Almanack

Racing Tips — All the Classics. Dozens and dozens of lucky dates to follow — for Trainers and Jockeys.

Football and Greyhounds too.

Gardening Guide — Better Everything. Bigger; better; more colour. Whatever you want! Lunar planting is the key.

Fish Attack — Anglers get the upper hand and catch more fish. Dates, times and species to fish are all here.

With Key Zodiac Sign dates of course.

A great New Year investment for you.
An inexpensive, fun gift for your friends.

Look for it at W. H. Smith, John Menzies, Martins and all good newsagents.